T0221733

Compiler Design: Principles, Techniques and Tools

Compiler Design: Principles, Techniques and Tools

Edited by
Terence Halsey

 Larsen & Keller
www.larsen-keller.com

Compiler Design: Principles, Techniques and Tools
Edited by Terence Halsey
ISBN: 978-1-63549-677-2 (Hardback)

 **Larsen & Keller**

Published by Larsen and Keller Education,
5 Penn Plaza,
19th Floor,
New York, NY 10001, USA

Cataloging-in-Publication Data

Compiler design : principles, techniques and tools / edited by Terence Halsey.
    p. cm.
Includes bibliographical references and index.
ISBN 978-1-63549-677-2
1. Compilers (Computer programs). 2. Computer software--Development.
I. Halsey, Terence.
QA76.76.C65 C66 2018
005.453--dc23

For more information regarding Larsen and Keller Education and its products, please visit the publisher's website www.larsen-keller.com

Table of Contents

Preface

A computer program that aids the process of transforming a source code language into another computer language is called compiler. It is used to create executable programs. Compiler design refers to the designing, planning, maintaining, and creating computer languages, by performing run-time organization, verifying code syntax, formatting outputs with respect to linkers and assemblers, and by generating efficient object codes. This book provides comprehensive insights into the field of compiler design. It aims to shed light on some of the unexplored aspects of the subject. The text includes topics which provide in-depth information about its techniques, principles and tools. This textbook is an essential guide for both academicians and those who wish to pursue this discipline further.

Given below is the chapter wise description of the book:

Chapter 1- A compiler converts source code to another computer language. Compilers help in the creation of an executable program. Compilers are also used to change the attributes of a computer program as an optimizing compiler is usually used to minimize the time required to run a program. This chapter is an overview of the subject matter incorporating all the major aspects of compiler design.

Chapter 2- The major components of compiler design are discussed in this chapter. They are lexical, syntax and semantic analysis. The process of translating characters into identifiable tokens is called lexical analysis whereas in syntax analysis or parsing, the strings of symbols are examined keeping formal grammar as a base. After parsing, semantic code is collected. This is called semantic analysis.

Chapter 3- Runtime system, like compiler, is a part of program execution. It is required to manage the sequence of work that gets performed, which is listed through programming language. It acts as a gateway between the running program and the runtime environment. The chapter closely examines the key concepts of compiler design to provide an extensive understanding of the subject.

Chapter 4- The code used by a compiler to represent a source code is referred to as intermediate representation. A good intermediate representation needs to be accurate so that it can represent the source code without losing any information. Intermediate representation is an interdisciplinary subject. It spreads to other fields as well. This chapter will provide a glimpse of related fields of intermediate representation briefly.

At the end, I would like to thank all those who dedicated their time and efforts for the successful completion of this book. I also wish to convey my gratitude towards my friends and family who supported me at every step.

Editor

Basics of Compiler Design

A compiler converts source code to another computer language. Compilers help in the creation of an executable program. Compilers are also used to change the attributes of a computer program as an optimizing compiler is usually used to minimize the time required to run a program. This chapter is an overview of the subject matter incorporating all the major aspects of compiler design.

Compilers

Compiler is a program which translates a program written in one language (the source language) to an equivalent program in other language (the target language). Usually the source language is a high level language like Java, C, Fortran etc. whereas the target language is machine code or "code" that a computer's processor understands. The source language is optimized for humans. It is more user-friendly, to some extent platform-independent. They are easier to read, write, and maintain and hence it is easy to avoid errors. Ultimately, programs written in a high-level language must be translated into machine language by a compiler. The target machine language is efficient for hardware but lacks readability.

- Translates from one representation of the program to another

- Typically from high level source code to low level machine code or object code

- Source code is normally optimized for human readability

    - Expressive: matches our notion of languages (and application?!)

    - Redundant to help avoid programming errors

- Machine code is optimized for hardware

    - Redundancy is reduced

    - Information about the intent is lost

Cross Compiler

A cross compiler is a compiler capable of creating executable code for a platform other than the one on which the compiler is running. For example, a compiler that runs on a Windows 7 PC but generates code that runs on Android smartphone is a cross compiler.

A cross compiler is necessary to compile for multiple platforms from one machine. A platform could be infeasible for a compiler to run on, such as for the microcontroller of an embedded system because those systems contain no operating system. In paravirtualization one machine runs many operating systems, and a cross compiler could generate an executable for each of them from one main source.

Cross compilers are not to be confused with source-to-source compilers. A cross compiler is for cross-platform software development of binary code, while a source-to-source compiler translates from one programming language to another in text code. Both are programming tools.

Uses of Cross Compilers

The fundamental use of a cross compiler is to separate the build environment from target environment. This is useful in a number of situations:

- Embedded computers where a device has extremely limited resources. For example, a microwave oven will have an extremely small computer to read its touchpad and door sensor, provide output to a digital display and speaker, and to control the machinery for cooking food. This computer will not be powerful enough to run a compiler, a file system, or a development environment. Since debugging and testing may also require more resources than are available on an embedded system, cross-compilation can be less involved and less prone to errors than native compilation.

- Compiling for multiple machines. For example, a company may wish to support several different versions of an operating system or to support several different operating systems. By using a cross compiler, a single build environment can be set up to compile for each of these targets.

- Compiling on a server farm. Similar to compiling for multiple machines, a complicated build that involves many compile operations can be executed across any machine that is free, regardless of its underlying hardware or the operating system version that it is running.

- Bootstrapping to a new platform. When developing software for a new platform, or the emulator of a future platform, one uses a cross compiler to compile necessary tools such as the operating system and a native compiler.

- Compiling native code for emulators for older now-obsolete platforms like the Commodore 64 or Apple II by enthusiasts who use cross compilers that run on a current platform (such as Aztec C's MS-DOS 6502 cross compilers running under Windows XP).

Use of virtual machines (such as Java's JVM) resolves some of the reasons for which cross compilers were developed. The virtual machine paradigm allows the same compiler output to be used across multiple target systems, although this is not always ideal because virtual machines are often slower and the compiled program can only be run on computers with that virtual machine.

Typically the hardware architecture differs (e.g. compiling a program destined for the MIPS architecture on an x86 computer) but cross-compilation is also applicable when only the operating system environment differs, as when compiling a FreeBSD program under Linux, or even just the system library, as when compiling programs with uClibc on a glibc host.

Canadian Cross

The Canadian Cross is a technique for building cross compilers for other machines. Given three machines A, B, and C, one uses machine A (e.g. running Windows XP on an IA-32 processor) to build a cross compiler that runs on machine B (e.g. running Mac OS X on an x86-64 processor) to create executables for machine C (e.g. running Android on an ARM processor). When using the Canadian Cross with GCC, there may be four compilers involved:

*   The *proprietary native Compiler for machine A (1)* (e.g. compiler from Microsoft Visual Studio) is used to build the *gcc native compiler for machine A (2)*.

*   The *gcc native compiler for machine A (2)* is used to build the *gcc cross compiler from machine A to machine B (3)*.

*   The *gcc cross compiler from machine A to machine B (3)* is used to build the *gcc cross compiler from machine B to machine C (4)*.

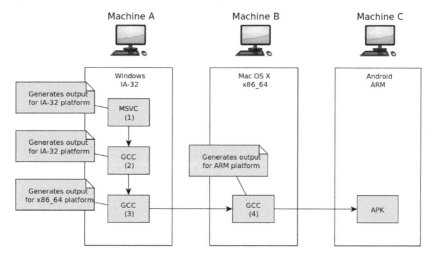

The end-result cross compiler (4) will not be able to run on build machine A; instead it would run on machine B to compile an application into executable code that would then be copied to machine C and executed on machine C.

For instance, NetBSD provides a POSIX Unix shell script named `build.sh` which will first build its own toolchain with the host's compiler; this, in turn, will be used to build the cross-compiler which will be used to build the whole system.

The term Canadian Cross came about because at the time that these issues were under discussion, Canada had three national political parties.

Timeline of Early Cross Compilers

*   1979 – ALGOL 68C generated ZCODE; this aided porting the compiler and other ALGOL 68 applications to alternate platforms. To compile the ALGOL 68C compiler required about 120kB of memory. With Z80 its 64kB memory is too small to actually compile the compiler. So for the Z80 the compiler itself had to be cross compiled from the larger CAP capability computer or an IBM System/370 mainframe.

GCC and Cross Compilation

GCC, a free software collection of compilers, can be set up to cross compile. It supports many platforms and languages.

GCC requires that a compiled copy of binutils be available for each targeted platform. Especially important is the GNU Assembler. Therefore, binutils first has to be compiled correctly with the switch `--target=some-target` sent to the configure script. GCC also has to be configured with the same --target option. GCC can then be run normally provided that the tools, which binutils creates, are available in the path, which can be done using the following (on UNIX-like operating systems with bash):

```
PATH=/path/to/binutils/bin:${PATH} make
```

Cross compiling GCC requires that a portion of the *target platform*'s C standard library be available on the *host platform*. The programmer may choose to compile the full C library, but this choice could be unreliable. The alternative is to use newlib, which is a small C library containing only the most essential components required to compile C source code.

The GNU autotools packages (i.e. autoconf, automake, and libtool) use the notion of a *build platform*, a *host platform*, and a *target platform*. The *build platform* is where the compiler is actually compiled. In most cases, build should be left undefined (it will default from host). The *host platform* is where the output artifacts from the compiler will be executed. The *target platform* is used when cross compiling cross compilers, it represents what type of object code the package itself will produce; otherwise the *target platform* setting is irrelevant. For example, consider cross-compiling a video game that will run on a Dreamcast. The machine where the game is compiled is the *host platform* while the Dreamcast is the *target platform*.

Another method popularly used by embedded Linux developers involves the combination of GCC compilers with specialized sandboxes like Scratchbox, scratchbox2, or PRoot. These tools create a "chrooted" sandbox where the programmer can build up necessary tools, libc, and libraries without having to set extra paths. Facilities are also provided to "deceive" the runtime so that it "believes" it is actually running on the intended target CPU (such as an ARM architecture); this allows configuration scripts and the like to run without error. Scratchbox runs more slowly by comparison to "non-chrooted" methods, and most tools that are on the host must be moved into Scratchbox to function.

Manx Aztec C Cross Compilers

Manx Software Systems, of Shrewsbury, New Jersey, produced C compilers beginning in the 1980s targeted at professional developers for a variety of platforms up to and including PCs and Macs.

Manx's Aztec C programming language was available for a variety of platforms including MS-DOS, Apple II, DOS 3.3 and ProDOS, Commodore 64, Macintosh 68XXX and Amiga.

From the 1980s and continuing throughout the 1990s until Manx Software Systems disappeared, the MS-DOS version of Aztec C was offered both as a native mode compiler or as a cross compiler for other platforms with different processors including the Commodore 64 and Apple II. Internet distributions still exist for Aztec C including their MS-DOS based cross compilers. They are still in use today.

Manx's Aztec C86, their native mode 8086 MS-DOS compiler, was also a cross compiler. Although it did not compile code for a different processor like their Aztec C65 6502 cross compilers for the Commodore 64 and Apple II, it created binary executables for then-legacy operating systems for the 16 bit 8086 family of processors.

When the IBM PC was first introduced it was available with a choice of operating systems, CP/M-86 and PC DOS being two of them. Aztec C86 was provided with link libraries for generating code for both IBM PC operating systems. Throughout the 1980s later versions of Aztec C86 (3.xx, 4.xx and 5.xx) added support for MS-DOS "transitory" versions 1 and 2 and which were less robust than the "baseline" MS-DOS version 3 and later which Aztec C86 targeted until its demise.

Finally, Aztec C86 provided C language developers with the ability to produce ROM-able "HEX" code which could then be transferred using a ROM Burner directly to an 8086 based processor. Paravirtualization may be more common today but the practice of creating low-level ROM code was more common per-capita during those years when device driver development was often done by application programmers for individual applications, and new devices amounted to a cottage industry. It was not uncommon for application programmers to interface directly with hardware without support from the manufacturer. This practice was similar to Embedded Systems Development today.

Thomas Fenwick and James Goodnow II were the two principal developers of Aztec-C. Fenwick later became notable as the author of the Microsoft Windows CE Kernel or NK ("New Kernel") as it was then called.

Microsoft C Cross Compilers

Early History – 1980s

Microsoft C (MSC) has a long history dating back to the 1980s. The first Microsoft C Compilers were made by the same company who made Lattice C and were rebranded by Microsoft as their own, until MSC 4 was released, which was the first version that Microsoft produced themselves.

In 1987 many developers started switching to Microsoft C, and many more would follow throughout the development of Microsoft Windows to its present state. Products like Clipper and later Clarion emerged that offered easy database application development by using cross language techniques, allowing part of their programs to be compiled with Microsoft C.

1987

C programs had long been linked with modules written in assembly language. Most C compilers (even current compilers) offer an assembly language pass (that can be tweaked for efficiency then linked to the rest of the program after assembling).

Compilers like Aztec-C converted everything to assembly language as a distinct pass and then assembled the code in a distinct pass, and were noted for their very efficient and small code, but by 1987 the optimizer built into Microsoft C was very good, and only "mission critical" parts of a program were usually considered for rewriting. In fact, C language programming had taken over as the "lowest-level" language, with programming becoming a multi-disciplinary growth industry and projects becoming larger, with programmers writing user interfaces and database interfaces in higher-level languages, and a need had emerged for cross language development that continues to this day.

By 1987, with the release of MSC 5.1, Microsoft offered a cross language development environment for MS-DOS. 16 bit binary object code written in assembly language (MASM) and Microsoft's other languages including Quick Basic, Pascal, and Fortran could be linked together into one program, in a process they called "Mixed Language Programming" and now "InterLanguage Calling". If BASIC was used in this mix, the main program needed to be in BASIC to support the internal run-time system that compiled BASIC required for garbage collection and its other managed operations that simulated a BASIC interpreter like QBasic in MS-DOS.

The calling convention for C code in particular was to pass parameters in "reverse order" on the stack and return values on the stack rather than in a processor register. There were other programming rules to make all the languages work together, but this particular rule persisted through the cross language development that continued throughout Windows 16 and 32 bit versions and in the development of programs for OS/2, and which persists to this day. It is known as the Pascal calling convention.

Another type of cross compilation that Microsoft C was used for during this time was in retail applications that require handheld devices like the Symbol Technologies PDT3100 (used to take inventory), which provided a link library targeted at an 8088 based barcode reader. The application was built on the host computer then transferred to the handheld device (via a serial cable) where it was run, similar to what is done today for that same market using Windows Mobile by companies like Motorola, who bought Symbol.

Early 1990s

Throughout the 1990s and beginning with MSC 6 (their first ANSI C compliant compiler) Microsoft re-focused their C compilers on the emerging Windows market, and also on OS/2 and in the development of GUI programs. Mixed language compatibility remained through MSC 6 on the MS-DOS side, but the API for Microsoft Windows 3.0 and 3.1 was written in MSC 6. MSC 6 was also extended to provide support for 32-bit assemblies and support for the emerging Windows for Workgroups and Windows NT which would form the foundation for Windows XP. A programming practice called a thunk was introduced to allow passing between 16 and 32 bit programs that took advantage of runtime binding (dynamic linking) rather than the static binding that was favoured in monolithic 16 bit MS-DOS applications. Static binding is still favoured by some native code developers but does not generally provide the degree of code reuse required by newer best practices like the Capability Maturity Model (CMM).

MS-DOS support was still provided with the release of Microsoft's first C++ Compiler, MSC 7, which was backwardly compatible with the C programming language and MS-DOS and supported both 16 bit and 32 bit code generation.

MSC took over where Aztec C86 left off. The market share for C compilers had turned to cross compilers which took advantage of the latest and greatest Windows features, offered C and C++ in a single bundle, and still supported MS-DOS systems that were already a decade old, and the smaller companies that produced compilers like Aztec C could no longer compete and either turned to niche markets like embedded systems or disappeared.

MS-DOS and 16 bit code generation support continued until MSC 8.00c which was bundled with Microsoft C++ and Microsoft Application Studio 1.5, the forerunner of Microsoft Visual Studio which is the cross development environment that Microsoft provide today.

Late 1990s

MSC 12 was released with Microsoft Visual Studio 6 and no longer provided support for MS-DOS 16 bit binaries, instead providing support for 32 bit console applications, but provided support for Windows 95 and Windows 98 code generation as well as for Windows NT. Link libraries were available for other processors that ran Microsoft Windows; a practice that Microsoft continues to this day.

MSC 13 was released with Visual Studio 2003, and MSC 14 was released with Visual Studio 2005, both of which still produce code for older systems like Windows 95, but which will produce code for several target platforms including the mobile market and the ARM architecture.

.NET and Beyond

In 2001 Microsoft developed the Common Language Runtime (CLR), which formed the core for their .NET Framework compiler in the Visual Studio IDE. This layer on the operating system which is in the API allows the mixing of development languages compiled across platforms that run the Windows operating system.

The .NET Framework runtime and CLR provide a mapping layer to the core routines for the processor and the devices on the target computer. The command-line C compiler in Visual Studio will compile native code for a variety of processors and can be used to build the core routines themselves.

Microsoft .NET applications for target platforms like Windows Mobile on the ARM architecture cross-compile on Windows machines with a variety of processors and Microsoft also offer emulators and remote deployment environments that require very little configuration, unlike the cross compilers in days gone by or on other platforms.

Runtime libraries, such as Mono, provide compatibility for cross-compiled .NET programs to other operating systems, such as Linux.

Libraries like Qt and its predecessors including XVT provide source code level cross development capability with other platforms, while still using Microsoft C to build the Windows versions. Other compilers like MinGW have also become popular in this area since they are more directly compatible with the Unixes that comprise the non-Windows side of software development allowing those developers to target all platforms using a familiar build environment.

Free Pascal

Free Pascal was developed from the beginning as a cross compiler. The compiler executable (ppcXXX where XXX is a target architecture) is capable of producing executables (or just object files if no internal linker exists, or even just assembly files if no internal assembler exists) for all OS of the same architecture. For example, ppc386 is capable of producing executables for i386-linux, i386-win32, i386-go32v2 (DOS) and all other OSes. For compiling to another architecture, however, a cross architecture version of the compiler must be built first. The resulting compiler executable would have additional 'ross' before the target architecture in its name. i.e. if the compiler is built to target x64, then the executable would be ppcrossx64.

To compile for a chosen architecture-OS, the compiler switch (for the compiler driver fpc) -P and -T can be used. This is also done when cross compiling the compiler itself, but is set via make option CPU_TARGET and OS_TARGET. GNU assembler and linker for the target platform is required if Free Pascal doesn't yet have internal version of the tools for the target platform.

Source-to-source Compiler

A source-to-source compiler, transcompiler or transpiler is a type of compiler that takes the source code of a program written in one programming language as its input and produces the equivalent source code in another programming language. A source-to-source compiler translates between programming languages that operate at approximately the same level of abstraction, while a traditional compiler translates from a higher level programming language to a lower level programming language. For example, a source-to-source compiler may perform a translation of a program from Pascal to C. An automatic parallelizing compiler will frequently take in a high level language program as an input and then transform the code and annotate it with parallel code annotations (e.g., OpenMP) or language constructs (e.g. Fortran's `forall` statements).

Another purpose of source-to-source-compiling is translating legacy code to use the next version of the underlying programming language or an API that breaks backward compatibility. It will perform automatic code refactoring which is useful when the programs to refactor are outside the control of the original implementer (for example, converting programs from Python 2 to Python 3, or converting programs from an old API to the new API) or when the size of the program makes it impractical or time consuming to refactor it by hand.

Transcompilers may either keep translated code as close to the source code as possible to ease development and debugging of the original source code, or may change the structure of the original code so much that the translated code does not look like the source code. There are also debugging utilities that map the transpiled source code back to the original code; for example, JavaScript source maps allow mapping of the JavaScript code executed by a web browser back to the original source in a transpiled-to-JavaScript language.

Examples of transcompiled languages include Closure Compiler, Coccinelle, CoffeeScript, Dart, Haxe, Nim, TypeScript and Emscripten.

History

One of the earliest programs of this kind was Digital Research's XLT86 in 1981, a program written by Gary Kildall, which translated .ASM source code for the Intel 8080 processor into .A86 source code for the Intel 8086. Using global data flow analysis on 8080 register usage, the translator would also optimize the output for code size and take care of calling conventions, so that CP/M-80 and MP/M-80 programs could be ported to the CP/M-86 and MP/M-86 platforms automatically. XLT86 itself was written in PL/I-80 and was available for CP/M-80 platforms as well as for DEC VMS (for VAX 11/750 or 11/780).

A similar, but much less sophisticated program was TRANS.COM, written by Tim Paterson in 1980 as part of 86-DOS. It could translate some Z80 assembly source code into .ASM source code for the 8086, but supported only a subset of opcodes, registers and modes, often still requiring significant manual correction and rework afterwards. Also it did not carry out any register and jump optimizations.

Porting a Codebase

When developers want to switch to a different language while retaining most of an existing codebase, it might be better to use a transcompiler compared to rewriting the whole software by hand. In this case, the code often needs manual correction because the automated translation might not work in all cases.

Tool	Source language	Target language	Comments
2to3 script	Python 2	Python 3	Even though 2to3 does its best at automating the translation process, further manual corrections are often needed.
Emscripten	LLVM bytecode	JavaScript	This allows running C/C++ codebases in a browser for example
Google Web Toolkit	Java program that uses a specific API	JavaScript	The Java code is a little bit constrained compared to normal Java code.
Js_of_ocaml of Ocsigen	OCaml	JavaScript	
J2Eif	Java	Eiffel	The resulting Eiffel code has classes and structures similar to the Java program but following Eiffel syntax and conventions.
C2Eif	C	Eiffel	The resulting Eiffel code has classes and structures that try to be as clean as possible. The tool is complete and relies on embedding the C and assembly code if it cannot translate it properly.

Transcompiler Pipelines

A transcompiler pipeline is what results from recursive transcompiling. By stringing together multiple layers of tech, with a transcompile step between each layer, technology can be repeatedly transformed, effectively creating a distributed language independent specification.

Xslt is a general purpose transform tool which can be used between many different technologies, to create such a derivative code pipeline.

Optimizing Compiler

In computing, an optimizing compiler is a compiler that tries to minimize or maximize some attributes of an executable computer program. The most common requirement is to minimize the time taken to execute a program; a less common one is to minimize the amount of memory occupied. The growth of portable computers has created a market for minimizing the power consumed by a program. Compiler optimization is generally implemented using a sequence of *optimizing transformations*, algorithms which take a program and transform it to produce a semantically equivalent output program that uses fewer resources.

It has been shown that some code optimization problems are NP-complete, or even undecidable. In practice, factors such as the programmer's willingness to wait for the compiler to complete its task place upper limits on the optimizations that a compiler implementor might provide. (Optimization is generally a very CPU- and memory-intensive process.) In the past, computer memory limitations were also a major factor in limiting which optimizations could be performed. Because of all these factors, optimization rarely produces "optimal" output in any sense, and in fact an "optimization" may impede performance in some cases; rather, they are heuristic methods for improving resource usage in typical programs.

Types of Optimization

Techniques used in optimization can be broken up among various *scopes* which can affect anything from a single statement to the entire program. Generally speaking, locally scoped techniques are easier to implement than global ones but result in smaller gains. Some examples of scopes include:

Peephole optimizations

> Usually performed late in the compilation process after machine code has been generated. This form of optimization examines a few adjacent instructions (like "looking through a peephole" at the code) to see whether they can be replaced by a single instruction or a shorter sequence of instructions. For instance, a multiplication of a value by 2 might be more efficiently executed by left-shifting the value or by adding the value to itself. (This example is also an instance of strength reduction.)

Local optimizations

> These only consider information local to a basic block. Since basic blocks have no control flow, these optimizations need very little analysis (saving time and reducing storage requirements), but this also means that no information is preserved across jumps.

Global optimizations

> These are also called "intraprocedural methods" and act on whole functions. This gives them more information to work with but often makes expensive computations necessary. Worst case assumptions have to be made when function calls occur or global variables are accessed (because little information about them is available).

Loop optimizations

> These act on the statements which make up a loop, such as a *for* loop (e.g., loop-invariant code motion). Loop optimizations can have a significant impact because many programs spend a large percentage of their time inside loops.

Prescient store optimizations

> Allow store operations to occur earlier than would otherwise be permitted in the context of threads and locks. The process needs some way of knowing ahead of time what value will be stored by the assignment that it should have followed. The purpose of this relaxation is to

allow compiler optimization to perform certain kinds of code rearrangement that preserve the semantics of properly synchronized programs.

Interprocedural, whole-program or link-time optimization

These analyze all of a program's source code. The greater quantity of information extracted means that optimizations can be more effective compared to when they only have access to local information (i.e., within a single function). This kind of optimization can also allow new techniques to be performed. For instance function inlining, where a call to a function is replaced by a copy of the function body.

Machine code optimization

These analyze the executable task image of the program after all of an executable machine code has been linked. Some of the techniques that can be applied in a more limited scope, such as macro compression (which saves space by collapsing common sequences of instructions), are more effective when the entire executable task image is available for analysis.

In addition to scoped optimizations there are two further general categories of optimization:

Programming language–independent vs language-dependent

Most high-level languages share common programming constructs and abstractions: decision (if, switch, case), looping (for, while, repeat.. until, do.. while), and encapsulation (structures, objects). Thus similar optimization techniques can be used across languages. However, certain language features make some kinds of optimizations difficult. For instance, the existence of pointers in C and C++ makes it difficult to optimize array accesses. However, languages such as PL/1 (that also supports pointers) nevertheless have available sophisticated optimizing compilers to achieve better performance in various other ways. Conversely, some language features make certain optimizations easier. For example, in some languages functions are not permitted to have side effects. Therefore, if a program makes several calls to the same function with the same arguments, the compiler can immediately infer that the function's result need be computed only once. In languages where functions are allowed to have side effects, another strategy is possible. The optimizer can determine which function has no side effects, and restrict such optimizations to side effect free functions. This optimization is only possible when the optimizer has access to the called function.

Machine independent vs machine dependent

Many optimizations that operate on abstract programming concepts (loops, objects, structures) are independent of the machine targeted by the compiler, but many of the most effective optimizations are those that best exploit special features of the target platform. E.g.: Instructions which do several things at once, such as decrement register and branch if not zero.

The following is an instance of a local machine dependent optimization. To set a register to 0, the obvious way is to use the constant '0' in an instruction that sets a register value to a constant. A less obvious way is to XOR a register with itself. It is up to the compiler to know which instruction variant to use. On many RISC machines, both instructions would be equally appropriate, since they would both be the same length and take the same time. On many other microprocessors such as the Intel x86 family, it turns out that the XOR variant is shorter and probably faster, as there will be no need to decode an immediate operand, nor use the internal "immediate operand register". (A potential problem with this is that XOR may introduce a data dependency on the previous value of the register, causing a pipeline stall. However, processors often have XOR of a register with itself as a special case that doesn't cause stalls.)

Factors Affecting Optimization

The machine itself

> Many of the choices about which optimizations can and should be done depend on the characteristics of the target machine. It is sometimes possible to parameterize some of these machine dependent factors, so that a single piece of compiler code can be used to optimize different machines just by altering the machine description parameters. GCC is a compiler which exemplifies this approach.

The architecture of the target CPU

> Number of CPU registers: To a certain extent, the more registers, the easier it is to optimize for performance. Local variables can be allocated in the registers and not on the stack. Temporary/intermediate results can be left in registers without writing to and reading back from memory.

- RISC vs CISC: CISC instruction sets often have variable instruction lengths, often have a larger number of possible instructions that can be used, and each instruction could take differing amounts of time. RISC instruction sets attempt to limit the variability in each of these: instruction sets are usually constant length, with few exceptions, there are usually fewer combinations of registers and memory operations, and the instruction issue rate (the number of instructions completed per time period, usually an integer multiple of the clock cycle) is usually constant in cases where memory latency is not a factor. There may be several ways of carrying out a certain task, with CISC usually offering more alternatives than RISC. Compilers have to know the relative costs among the various instructions and choose the best instruction sequence.

- Pipelines: A pipeline is essentially a CPU broken up into an assembly line. It allows use of parts of the CPU for different instructions by breaking up the execution of instructions into various stages: instruction decode, address decode, memory fetch, register fetch, compute, register store, etc. One instruction could be in the register store stage, while another could be in the register fetch stage. Pipeline conflicts occur when an instruction in one stage of the pipeline depends on the result of another instruction ahead of it in the pipeline but not yet completed. Pipeline conflicts can lead to pipeline stalls: where the CPU wastes cycles waiting for a conflict to resolve.

> Compilers can *schedule*, or reorder, instructions so that pipeline stalls occur less frequently.

- Number of functional units: Some CPUs have several ALUs and FPUs. This allows them to execute multiple instructions simultaneously. There may be restrictions on which instructions can pair with which other instructions ("pairing" is the simultaneous execution of two or more instructions), and which functional unit can execute which instruction. They also have issues similar to pipeline conflicts.

Here again, instructions have to be scheduled so that the various functional units are fully fed with instructions to execute.

The architecture of the machine

- Cache size (256 kiB–12 MiB) and type (direct mapped, 2-/4-/8-/16-way associative, fully associative): Techniques such as inline expansion and loop unrolling may increase the size of the generated code and reduce code locality. The program may slow down drastically if a highly utilized section of code (like inner loops in various algorithms) suddenly cannot fit in the cache. Also, caches which are not fully associative have higher chances of cache collisions even in an unfilled cache.

- Cache/Memory transfer rates: These give the compiler an indication of the penalty for cache misses. This is used mainly in specialized applications.

Intended use of the generated code

Debugging

While writing an application, a programmer will recompile and test often, and so compilation must be fast. This is one reason most optimizations are deliberately avoided during the test/debugging phase. Also, program code is usually "stepped through" using a symbolic debugger, and optimizing transformations, particularly those that reorder code, can make it difficult to relate the output code with the line numbers in the original source code. This can confuse both the debugging tools and the programmers using them.

General purpose use

Prepackaged software is very often expected to be executed on a variety of machines and CPUs that may share the same instruction set, but have different timing, cache or memory characteristics. So, the code may not be tuned to any particular CPU, or may be tuned to work best on the most popular CPU and yet still work acceptably well on other CPUs.

Special-purpose use

If the software is compiled to be used on one or a few very similar machines, with known characteristics, then the compiler can heavily tune the generated code to those specific machines (if such options are available). Important special cases include code designed for parallel and vector processors, for which special parallelizing compilers are employed.

Embedded systems

These are a common case of special-purpose use. Embedded software can be tightly tuned to an exact CPU and memory size. Also, system cost or reliability may be more important than the code's speed. So, for example, compilers for embedded software usually offer options that reduce code size at the expense of speed, because memory is the main cost of an embedded computer. The code's timing may need to be predictable, rather than as fast as possible, so code caching might be disabled, along with compiler optimizations that require it.

Common Themes

To a large extent, compiler optimization techniques have the following themes, which sometimes conflict.

Optimize the common case

> The common case may have unique properties that allow a *fast path* at the expense of a *slow path*. If the fast path is taken most often, the result is better overall performance.

Avoid redundancy

> Reuse results that are already computed and store them for later use, instead of recomputing them.

Less code

> Remove unnecessary computations and intermediate values. Less work for the CPU, cache, and memory usually results in faster execution. Alternatively, in embedded systems, less code brings a lower product cost.

Fewer jumps by using *straight line code*, also called *branch-free code*

> Less complicated code. Jumps (conditional or unconditional branches) interfere with the prefetching of instructions, thus slowing down code. Using inlining or loop unrolling can reduce branching, at the cost of increasing binary file size by the length of the repeated code. This tends to merge several basic blocks into one.

Locality

> Code and data that are accessed closely together in time should be placed close together in memory to increase spatial locality of reference.

Exploit the memory hierarchy

> Accesses to memory are increasingly more expensive for each level of the memory hierarchy, so place the most commonly used items in registers first, then caches, then main memory, before going to disk.

Parallelize

> Reorder operations to allow multiple computations to happen in parallel, either at the instruction, memory, or thread level.

More precise information is better

> The more precise the information the compiler has, the better it can employ any or all of these optimization techniques.

Runtime metrics can help

Information gathered during a test run can be used in profile-guided optimization. Information gathered at runtime (ideally with minimal overhead) can be used by a JIT compiler to dynamically improve optimization.

Strength reduction

Replace complex or difficult or expensive operations with simpler ones. For example, replacing division by a constant with multiplication by its reciprocal, or using induction variable analysis to replace multiplication by a loop index with addition.

Specific Techniques

Loop Optimizations

Some optimization techniques primarily designed to operate on loops include

Induction variable analysis

Roughly, if a variable in a loop is a simple linear function of the index variable, such as j := 4*i + 1, it can be updated appropriately each time the loop variable is changed. This is a strength reduction, and also may allow the index variable's definitions to become dead code. This information is also useful for bounds-checking elimination and dependence analysis, among other things.

Loop fission or loop distribution

Loop fission attempts to break a loop into multiple loops over the same index range but each taking only a part of the loop's body. This can improve locality of reference, both of the data being accessed in the loop and the code in the loop's body.

Loop fusion or loop combining or loop ramming or loop jamming

Another technique which attempts to reduce loop overhead. When two adjacent loops would iterate the same number of times (whether or not that number is known at compile time), their bodies can be combined as long as they make no reference to each other's data.

Loop inversion

This technique changes a standard *while* loop into a *do/while* (also known as *repeat/until*) loop wrapped in an *if* conditional, reducing the number of jumps by two, for cases when the loop is executed. Doing so duplicates the condition check (increasing the size of the code) but is more efficient because jumps usually cause a pipeline stall. Additionally, if the initial condition is known at compile-time and is known to be side-effect-free, the *if* guard can be skipped.

Loop interchange

These optimizations exchange inner loops with outer loops. When the loop variables index into an array, such a transformation can improve locality of reference, depending on the array's layout.

Loop-invariant code motion

> If a quantity is computed inside a loop during every iteration, and its value is the same for each iteration, it can vastly improve efficiency to hoist it outside the loop and compute its value just once before the loop begins. This is particularly important with the address-calculation expressions generated by loops over arrays. For correct implementation, this technique must be used with loop inversion, because not all code is safe to be hoisted outside the loop.

Loop nest optimization

> Some pervasive algorithms such as matrix multiplication have very poor cache behavior and excessive memory accesses. Loop nest optimization increases the number of cache hits by performing the operation over small blocks and by using a loop interchange.

Loop reversal

> Loop reversal reverses the order in which values are assigned to the index variable. This is a subtle optimization which can help eliminate dependencies and thus enable other optimizations. Furthermore, on some architectures, loop reversal contributes to smaller code, as when the loop index is being decremented, the condition that needs to be met in order for the running program to exit the loop is a comparison with zero. This is often a special, parameter-less instruction, unlike a comparison with a number, which needs the number to compare to. Therefore, the amount of bytes needed to store the parameter is saved by using the loop reversal. Additionally, if the comparison number exceeds the size of word of the platform, in standard loop order, multiple instructions would need to be executed in order to evaluate the comparison, which is not the case with loop reversal.

Loop unrolling

> Unrolling duplicates the body of the loop multiple times, in order to decrease the number of times the loop condition is tested and the number of jumps, which hurt performance by impairing the instruction pipeline. A "fewer jumps" optimization. Completely unrolling a loop eliminates all overhead, but requires that the number of iterations be known at compile time.

Loop splitting

> Loop splitting attempts to simplify a loop or eliminate dependencies by breaking it into multiple loops which have the same bodies but iterate over different contiguous portions of the index range. A useful special case is *loop peeling*, which can simplify a loop with a problematic first iteration by performing that iteration separately before entering the loop.

Loop unswitching

> Unswitching moves a conditional from inside a loop to outside the loop by duplicating the loop's body inside each of the if and else clauses of the conditional.

Software pipelining

> The loop is restructured in such a way that work done in an iteration is split into several parts and done over several iterations. In a tight loop this technique hides the latency between loading and using values.

Automatic parallelization

> A loop is converted into multi-threaded or vectorized (or even both) code in order to utilize multiple processors simultaneously in a shared-memory multiprocessor (SMP) machine, including multi-core machines.

Data-flow Optimizations

Data-flow optimizations, based on data-flow analysis, primarily depend on how certain properties of data are propagated by control edges in the control flow graph. Some of these include:

Common subexpression elimination

> In the expression (a + b) - (a + b)/4, "common subexpression" refers to the duplicated (a + b). Compilers implementing this technique realize that (a + b) won't change, and as such, only calculate its value once.

Constant folding and propagation

> replacing expressions consisting of constants (e.g., 3 + 5) with their final value (8) at compile time, rather than doing the calculation in run-time. Used in most modern languages.

Induction variable recognition and elimination

Alias classification and pointer analysis

> in the presence of pointers, it is difficult to make any optimizations at all, since potentially any variable can have been changed when a memory location is assigned to. By specifying which pointers can alias which variables, unrelated pointers can be ignored.

Dead store elimination

> removal of assignments to variables that are not subsequently read, either because the lifetime of the variable ends or because of a subsequent assignment that will overwrite the first value.

SSA-based Optimizations

These optimizations are intended to be done after transforming the program into a special form called static single assignment, in which every variable is assigned in only one place. Although some function without SSA, they are most effective with SSA. Many optimizations listed in other sections also benefit with no special changes, such as register allocation.

Global value numbering

GVN eliminates redundancy by constructing a value graph of the program, and then determining which values are computed by equivalent expressions. GVN is able to identify some redundancy that common subexpression elimination cannot, and vice versa.

Sparse conditional constant propagation

Combines constant propagation, constant folding, and dead code elimination, and improves upon what is possible by running them separately. This optimization symbolically executes the program, simultaneously propagating constant values and eliminating portions of the control flow graph that this makes unreachable.

Code Generator Optimizations

Register allocation

The most frequently used variables should be kept in processor registers for fastest access. To find which variables to put in registers an interference-graph is created. Each variable is a vertex and when two variables are used at the same time (have an intersecting liverange) they have an edge between them. This graph is colored using for example Chaitin's algorithm using the same number of colors as there are registers. If the coloring fails one variable is "spilled" to memory and the coloring is retried.

Instruction selection

Most architectures, particularly CISC architectures and those with many addressing modes, offer several different ways of performing a particular operation, using entirely different sequences of instructions. The job of the instruction selector is to do a good job overall of choosing which instructions to implement which operators in the low-level intermediate representation with. For example, on many processors in the 68000 family and on the x86 architecture, complex addressing modes can be used in statements like "lea 25(a1,d5*4), a0", allowing a single instruction to perform a significant amount of arithmetic with less storage.

Instruction scheduling

Instruction scheduling is an important optimization for modern pipelined processors, which avoids stalls or bubbles in the pipeline by clustering instructions with no dependencies together, while being careful to preserve the original semantics.

Rematerialization

Rematerialization recalculates a value instead of loading it from memory, preventing a memory access. This is performed in tandem with register allocation to avoid spills.

Code factoring

If several sequences of code are identical, or can be parameterized or reordered to be identical, they can be replaced with calls to a shared subroutine. This can often share code for subroutine set-up and sometimes tail-recursion.

Trampolines

> Many CPUs have smaller subroutine call instructions to access low memory. A compiler can save space by using these small calls in the main body of code. Jump instructions in low memory can access the routines at any address. This multiplies space savings from code factoring.

Reordering computations

> Based on integer linear programming, restructuring compilers enhance data locality and expose more parallelism by reordering computations. Space-optimizing compilers may re-order code to lengthen sequences that can be factored into subroutines.

Functional language optimizations

Although many of these also apply to non-functional languages, they either originate in, are most easily implemented in, or are particularly critical in functional languages such as Lisp and ML.

Removing recursion

> Recursion is often expensive, as a function call consumes stack space and involves some overhead related to parameter passing and flushing the instruction cache. Tail recursive algorithms can be converted to iteration, which does not have call overhead and uses a constant amount of stack space, through a process called tail recursion elimination or tail call optimization. Some functional languages (e.g., Scheme and Erlang) mandate that tail calls be optimized by a conforming implementation, due to their prevalence in these languages.

Deforestation (data structure fusion)

> Because of the high level nature by which data structures are specified in functional languages such as Haskell, it is possible to combine several recursive functions which produce and consume some temporary data structure so that the data is passed directly without wasting time constructing the data structure.

Other Optimizations

Bounds-checking elimination

> Many languages, for example Java, enforce bounds checking of all array accesses. This is a severe performance bottleneck on certain applications such as scientific code. Bounds-checking elimination allows the compiler to safely remove bounds checking in many situations where it can determine that the index must fall within valid bounds, for example if it is a simple loop variable.

Branch offset optimization (machine dependent)

> Choose the shortest branch displacement that reaches target

Code-block reordering

> Code-block reordering alters the order of the basic blocks in a program in order to reduce conditional branches and improve locality of reference.

Dead code elimination

> Removes instructions that will not affect the behaviour of the program, for example definitions which have no uses, called dead code. This reduces code size and eliminates unnecessary computation.

Factoring out of invariants

> If an expression is carried out both when a condition is met and is not met, it can be written just once outside of the conditional statement. Similarly, if certain types of expressions (e.g., the assignment of a constant into a variable) appear inside a loop, they can be moved out of it because their effect will be the same no matter if they're executed many times or just once. Also known as total redundancy elimination. A more powerful optimization is partial redundancy elimination (PRE).

Inline expansion or macro expansion

> When some code invokes a procedure, it is possible to directly insert the body of the procedure inside the calling code rather than transferring control to it. This saves the overhead related to procedure calls, as well as providing great opportunity for many different parameter-specific optimizations, but comes at the cost of space; the procedure body is duplicated each time the procedure is called inline. Generally, inlining is useful in performance-critical code that makes a large number of calls to small procedures. A "fewer jumps" optimization. The statements of imperative programming languages are also an example of such an optimization. Although statements could be implemented with function calls they are almost always implemented with code inlining.

Jump threading

> In this pass, consecutive conditional jumps predicated entirely or partially on the same condition are merged.
>
> ```
> E.g., if (c) { foo; } if (c) { bar; } to if (c) { foo; bar; },
>
> and if (c) { foo; } if (!c) { bar; } to if (c) { foo; } else { bar; }.
> ```

Macro Compression

> A space optimization that recognizes common sequences of code, creates subprograms ("code macros") that contain the common code, and replaces the occurrences of the common code sequences with calls to the corresponding subprograms. This is most effectively done as a machine code optimization, when all the code is present. The technique was first used to conserve space in an interpretive byte stream used in an implementation of Macro Spitbol on microcomputers. The problem of determining an optimal set of macros that minimizes the space required by a given code segment is known to be NP-complete, but efficient heuristics attain near-optimal results.

Reduction of cache collisions

> (e.g., by disrupting alignment within a page)

Stack height reduction

> Rearrange expression tree to minimize resources needed for expression evaluation.

Test reordering

> If we have two tests that are the condition for something, we can first deal with the simpler tests (e.g. comparing a variable to something) and only then with the complex tests (e.g., those that require a function call). This technique complements lazy evaluation, but can be used only when the tests are not dependent on one another. Short-circuiting semantics can make this difficult.

Interprocedural Optimizations

Interprocedural optimization works on the entire program, across procedure and file boundaries. It works tightly with intraprocedural counterparts, carried out with the cooperation of a local part and global part. Typical interprocedural optimizations are: procedure inlining, interprocedural dead code elimination, interprocedural constant propagation, and procedure reordering. As usual, the compiler needs to perform interprocedural analysis before its actual optimizations. Interprocedural analyses include alias analysis, array access analysis, and the construction of a call graph.

Interprocedural optimization is common in modern commercial compilers from SGI, Intel, Microsoft, and Sun Microsystems. For a long time the open source GCC was criticized for a lack of powerful interprocedural analysis and optimizations, though this is now improving. Another open source compiler with full analysis and optimization infrastructure is Open64.

Due to the extra time and space required by interprocedural analysis, most compilers do not perform it by default. Users must use compiler options explicitly to tell the compiler to enable interprocedural analysis and other expensive optimizations.

Problems with Optimization

Early in the history of compilers, compiler optimizations were not as good as hand-written ones. As compiler technologies have improved, good compilers can often generate better code than human programmers, and good post pass optimizers can improve highly hand-optimized code even further. For RISC CPU architectures, and even more so for VLIW hardware, compiler optimization is the key for obtaining efficient code, because RISC instruction sets are so compact that it is hard for a human to manually schedule or combine small instructions to get efficient results. Indeed, these architectures were designed to rely on compiler writers for adequate performance.

However, optimizing compilers are by no means perfect. There is no way that a compiler can guarantee that, for all program source code, the fastest (or smallest) possible equivalent compiled program is output; such a compiler is fundamentally impossible because it would solve the halting problem (assuming Turing completeness).

This may be proven by considering a call to a function, foo(). This function returns nothing and does not have side effects (no I/O, does not modify global variables and "live" data structures, etc.).

The fastest possible equivalent program would be simply to eliminate the function call. However, if the function foo() in fact does *not* return, then the program with the call to foo() would be different from the program without the call; the optimizing compiler will then have to determine this by solving the halting problem.

Additionally, there are a number of other more practical issues with optimizing compiler technology:

- Optimizing compilers focus on relatively shallow constant-factor performance improvements and do not typically improve the algorithmic complexity of a solution. For example, a compiler will not change an implementation of bubble sort to use mergesort instead.

- Compilers usually have to support a variety of conflicting objectives, such as cost of implementation, compilation speed and quality of generated code.

- A compiler typically only deals with a part of a program at a time, often the code contained within a single file or module; the result is that it is unable to consider contextual information that can only be obtained by processing the other files.

- The overhead of compiler optimization: Any extra work takes time; whole-program optimization is time consuming for large programs.

- The often complex interaction between optimization phases makes it difficult to find an optimal sequence in which to execute the different optimization phases.

Work to improve optimization technology continues. One approach is the use of so-called post-pass optimizers (some commercial versions of which date back to mainframe software of the late 1970s). These tools take the executable output by an "optimizing" compiler and optimize it even further. Post pass optimizers usually work on the assembly language or machine code level (contrast with compilers that optimize intermediate representations of programs). The performance of post pass compilers are limited by the fact that much of the information available in the original source code is not always available to them.

As processor performance continues to improve at a rapid pace, while memory bandwidth improves more slowly, optimizations that reduce memory bandwidth requirements (even at the cost of making the processor execute relatively more instructions) will become more useful. Examples of this, already mentioned above, include loop nest optimization and rematerialization.

History

Early compilers of the 1960s were often primarily concerned with simply compiling code correctly or efficiently – compile times were a major concern. One of the earliest notable optimizing compilers was that for BLISS (1970), which was described in *The Design of an Optimizing Compiler* (1975). By the 1980s optimizing compilers were sufficiently effective that programming in assembly language declined, and by the late 1990s for even performance sensitive code, optimizing compilers exceeded the performance of human experts. This co-evolved with the development of RISC chips and advanced processor features such as instruction scheduling and speculative execution which were designed to be targeted by optimizing compilers, rather than by human-written assembly code.

Process of Compiler

The high level languages and machine languages differ in level of abstraction. At machine level we deal with memory locations, registers whereas these resources are never accessed in high level languages. But the level of abstraction differs from language to language and some languages are farther from machine code than others

- Goals of translation

- Good performance for the generated code

Good performance for generated code: The metric for the quality of the generated code is the ratio between the size of handwritten code and compiled machine code for same program. A better compiler is one which generates smaller code. For optimizing compilers this ratio will be lesser.

- Good compile time performance

Good compile time performance: A handwritten machine code is more efficient than a compiled code in terms of the performance it produces. In other words, the program handwritten in machine code will run faster than compiled code. If a compiler produces a code which is 20-30% slower than the handwritten code then it is considered to be acceptable. In addition to this, the compiler itself must run fast (compilation time must be proportional to program size).

- Maintainable code

- High level of abstraction

- Correctness is a very important issue.

Correctness: A compiler's most important goal is correctness - all valid programs must compile correctly. How do we check if a compiler is correct i.e. whether a compiler for a programming language generates correct machine code for programs in the language. The complexity of writing a correct compiler is a major limitation on the amount of optimization that can be done.

Can compilers be proven to be correct? Very tedious!

- However, the correctness has an implication on the development cost

Many modern compilers share a common 'two stage' design. The "front end" translates the source language or the high level program into an intermediate representation. The second stage is the "back end", which works with the internal representation to produce code in the output language which is a low level code. The higher the abstraction a compiler can support, the better it is.

The Big Picture

- Compiler is part of program development environment

- The other typical components of this environment are editor, assembler, linker, loader, debugger, profiler etc.

- The compiler (and all other tools) must support each other for easy program development

All development systems are essentially a combination of many tools. For compiler, the other tools are debugger, assembler, linker, loader, profiler, editor etc. If these tools have support for each other than the program development becomes a lot easier.

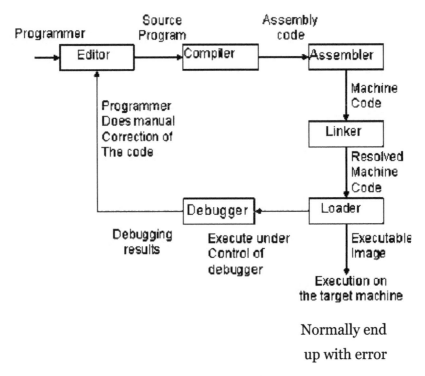

This is how the various tools work in coordination to make programming easier and better. They all have a specific task to accomplish in the process, from writing a code to compiling it and running/debugging it. If debugged then do manual correction in the code if needed, after getting debugging results. It is the combined contribution of these tools that makes programming a lot easier and efficient.

How to Translate Easily?

In order to translate a high level code to a machine code one needs to go step by step, with each step doing a particular task and passing out its output for the next step in the form of another program representation. The steps can be parse tree generation, high level intermediate code generation, low level intermediate code generation, and then the machine language conversion. As the translation proceeds the representation becomes more and more machine specific, increasingly dealing with registers, memory locations etc.

- Translate in steps. Each step handles a reasonably simple, logical, and well defined task

- Design a series of program representations

- Intermediate representations should be amenable to program manipulation of various kinds (type checking, optimization, code generation etc.)

- Representations become more machine specific and less language specific as the translation proceeds

The First Few Steps

The first few steps of compilation like lexical, syntax and semantic analysis can be understood by drawing analogies to the human way of comprehending a natural language. The first step in understanding a natural language will be to recognize characters, i.e. the upper and lower case alphabets, punctuation marks, alphabets, digits, white spaces etc. Similarly the compiler has to recognize the characters used in a programming language. The next step will be to recognize the words which come from a dictionary. Similarly the programming language have a dictionary as well as rules to construct words (numbers, identifiers etc).

- The first step is recognizing/knowing alphabets of a language. For example

  - English text consists of lower and upper case alphabets, digits, punctuations and white spaces

  - Written programs consist of characters from the ASCII characters set (normally 9-13, 32-126)

- The next step to understand the sentence is recognizing words (lexical analysis)

  - English language words can be found in dictionaries

  - Programming languages have a dictionary (keywords etc.) and rules for constructing words (identifiers, numbers etc.)

Lexical Analysis

- Recognizing words is not completely trivial. For example:

  - ist his ase nte nce?

- Therefore, we must know what the word separators are

- The language must define rules for breaking a sentence into a sequence of words.

- Normally white spaces and punctuations are word separators in languages.

- In programming languages a character from a different class may also be treated as word separator.

- The lexical analyzer breaks a sentence into a sequence of words or tokens:

  - If a == b then a = 1 ; else a = 2 ;- Sequence of words (total 14 words) if a == b then a = 1 ; else a = 2 ;

In simple words, lexical analysis is the process of identifying the words from an input string of characters, which may be handled more easily by a parser. These words must be separated by some predefined delimiter or there may be some rules imposed by the language for breaking the sentence into tokens or words which are then passed on to the next phase of syntax analysis. In programming languages, a character from a different class may also be considered as a word separator.

The Next Step

- Once the words are understood, the next step is to understand the structure of the sentence

- The process is known as syntax checking or parsing

Syntax analysis (also called as parsing) is a process of imposing a hierarchical (tree like) structure on the token stream. It is basically like generating sentences for the language using language specific grammatical rules as we have in our natural language Ex. sentence ¦subject + object + subject The example drawn above shows how a sentence in English (a natural language) can be broken down into a tree form depending on the construct of the sentence.

Parsing

Just like a natural language, a programming language also has a set of grammatical rules and hence can be broken down into a parse tree by the parser. It is on this parse tree that the further steps of semantic analysis are carried out. This is also used during generation of the intermediate language code. Yacc (yet another compiler compiler) is a program that generates parsers in the C programming language.

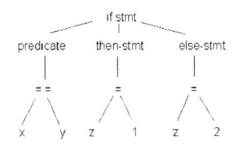

Understanding the Meaning

- Once the sentence structure is understood we try to understand the meaning of the sentence (semantic analysis)

- Example: Prateek said Nitin left his assignment at home

- What does his refer to? Prateek or Nitin ?

- Even worse case

Amit said Amit left his assignment at home

- How many Amits are there? Which one left the assignment?

Semantic analysis is the process of examining the statements and to make sure that they make sense. During the semantic analysis, the types, values, and other required information about statements are recorded, checked, and transformed appropriately to make sure the program makes sense. Ideally there should be no ambiguity in the grammar of the language. Each sentence should have just one meaning.

Semantic Analysis

- Too hard for compilers. They do not have capabilities similar to human understanding

- However, compilers do perform analysis to understand the meaning and catch inconsistencies

- Programming languages define strict rules to avoid such ambiguities

```
{ int Amit = 3;

    { int Amit = 4;

    cout << Amit;

    }

}
```

Since it is too hard for a compiler to do semantic analysis, the programming languages define strict rules to avoid ambiguities and make the analysis easier. In the code written above, there is a clear demarcation between the two instances of Amit. This has been done by putting one outside the scope of other so that the compiler knows that these two Amit are different by the virtue of their different scopes.

More on Semantic Analysis

- Compilers perform many other checks besides variable bindings

- Type checking Amit left her work at home

- There is a type mismatch between her and Amit . Presumably Amit is a male. And they are not the same person.

From this we can draw an analogy with a programming statement. In the statement:

double y = "Hello World"; The semantic analysis would reveal that "Hello World" is a string, and y is of type double, which is a type mismatch and hence, is wrong.

Compiler Structure Once Again

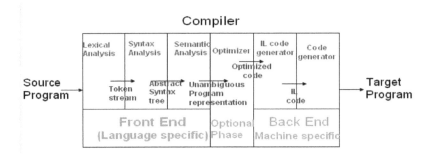

Till now we have conceptualized the front end of the compiler with its 3 phases, viz. Lexical Analysis, Syntax Analysis and Semantic Analysis; and the work done in each of the three phases.

Front End Phases

- Lexical Analysis
  - Recognize tokens and ignore white spaces, comments

  - Error reporting
  - Model using regular expressions
  - Recognize using Finite State Automata

Lexical analysis is based on the finite state automata and hence finds the lexicons from the input on the basis of corresponding regular expressions. If there is some input which it can't recognize then it generates error. In the above example, the delimiter is a blank space. The lexical analyzer recognizes identifiers, numbers, brackets etc.

Syntax Analysis

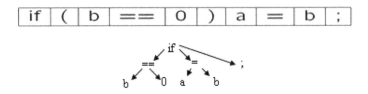

- Error reporting and recovery

- Model using context free grammars

- Recognize using Push down automata/Table Driven Parsers

Syntax Analysis is modeled on the basis of context free grammars. Programming languages can be written using context free grammars. Based on the rules of the grammar, a syntax tree can be made from a correct code of the language. A code written in a CFG is recognized using Push Down Automata. If there is any error in the syntax of the code then an error is generated by the compiler. Some compilers also tell that what exactly is the error, if possible.

Semantic Analysis

- Check semantics

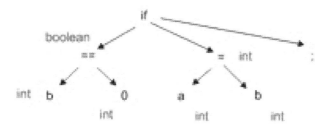

- Error reporting

- Disambiguate overloaded operators

- Type coercion

- Static checking

    - Type checking

    - Control flow checking

    - Unique ness checking

    - Name checks

Semantic analysis should ensure that the code is unambiguous. Also it should do the type checking wherever needed. Ex. int y = "Hi"; should generate an error. Type coercion can be explained by the following example:- int y = 5.6 + 1; The actual value of y used will be 6 since it is an integer. The compiler knows that since y is an instance of an integer it cannot have the value of 6.6 so it down-casts its value to the greatest integer less than 6.6. This is called type coercion.

Code Optimization

- No strong counter part with English, but is similar to editing/précis writing

- Automatically modify programs so that they

    - Run faster

    - Use less resources (memory, registers, space, fewer fetches etc.)

- Some common optimizations

  - Common sub-expression elimination

  - Copy propagation

  - Dead code elimination

  - Code motion

  - Strength reduction

  - Constant folding

- Example: x = 15 * 3 is transformed to x = 45

There is no strong counterpart in English, this is similar to precise writing where one cuts down the redundant words. It basically cuts down the redundancy. We modify the compiled code to make it more efficient such that it can - Run faster - Use less resources, such as memory, register, space, fewer fetches etc.

Example of Optimizations

PI = 3.14159	3A+4M+1D+2E
Area = 4 * PI * R^2	
Volume = (4/3) * PI * R^3	

X = 3.14159 * R * R	3A+5M
Area = 4 * X	
Volume = 1.33 * X * R	

Area = 4 * 3.14159 * R * R 2A+4M+1D Volume = (Area / 3) * R	2A+4M+1D

Area = 12.56636 * R * R	2A+3M+1D
Volume = (Area /3) * R	

X = R * R	3A+4M
A : assignment	M : multiplication
D : division	E : exponent

Example: see the following code,

```
int x = 2;

int y = 3;

int *array[5];

for (i=0; i<5;i++)

        *array[i] = x + y;
```

Because x and y are invariant and do not change inside of the loop, their addition doesn't need to be performed for each loop iteration. Almost any good compiler optimizes the code. An optimizer moves the addition of x and y outside the loop, thus creating a more efficient loop. Thus, the optimized code in this case could look like the following:

```
int x = 5;

int y = 7;

int z = x + y;

int *array[10];

for (i=0; i<5;i++)

        *array[i] = z;
```

Code Generation

- Usually a two step process

    - Generate intermediate code from the semantic representation of the program

    - Generate machine code from the intermediate code

- The advantage is that each phase is simple

- Requires design of intermediate language

- Most compilers perform translation between successive intermediate representations

- Intermediate languages are generally ordered in decreasing level of abstraction from highest (source) to lowest (machine)

- However, typically the one after the intermediate code generation is the most important

The final phase of the compiler is generation of the relocatable target code. First of all, Intermediate code is generated from the semantic representation of the source program, and this intermediate code is used to generate machine code.

Intermediate Code Generation

- Abstraction at the source level identifiers, operators, expressions, statements, conditionals, iteration, functions (user defined, system defined or libraries)

- Abstraction at the target level memory locations, registers, stack, opcodes, addressing modes, system libraries, interface to the operating systems

- Code generation is mapping from source level abstractions to target machine abstractions

- Map identifiers to locations (memory/storage allocation)

- Explicate variable accesses (change identifier reference to relocatable/absolute address

- Map source operators to opcodes or a sequence of opcodes

- Convert conditionals and iterations to a test/jump or compare instructions

- Layout parameter passing protocols: locations for parameters, return values, layout of activations frame etc.

- Interface calls to library, runtime system, operating systems

By the very definition of an intermediate language it must be at a level of abstraction which is in the middle of the high level source language and the low level target (machine) language. Design of the intermediate language is important. The IL should satisfy 2 main properties :

- easy to produce, and

- easy to translate into target language.

Thus it must not only relate to identifiers, expressions, functions & classes but also to opcodes, registers, etc. Then it must also map one abstraction to the other.

These are some of the things to be taken care of in the intermediate code generation.

Post Translation Optimizations

- Algebraic transformations and re-ordering

  - Remove/simplify operations like

    . Multiplication by 1

    . Multiplication by 0

    . Addition with 0

- Reorder instructions based on

  - Commutative properties of operators

  - For example x+y is same as y+x (always?)

- Instruction selection

  - Addressing mode selection

  - Opcode selection

  - Peephole optimization

Some of the different optimization methods are :

1) Constant Folding - replacing y= 5+7 with y=12 or y=x*0 with y=0

2) Dead Code Elimination - e.g.,

If (false)

   a = 1;

else

   a = 2;

with a = 2;

3) Peephole Optimization - a machine-dependent optimization that makes a pass through low-level assembly-like instruction sequences of the program(called a peephole), and replacing them with a faster (usually shorter) sequences by removing redundant register loads and stores if possible.

4) Flow of Control Optimizations

5) Strength Reduction - replacing more expensive expressions with cheaper ones - like pow(x,2) with x*x

6) Common Sub expression elimination - like a = b*c, f= b*c*d with temp = b*c, a= temp, f= temp*d;

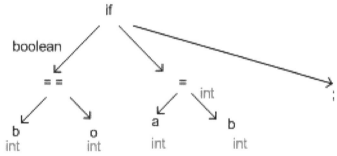

Intermediate code generation

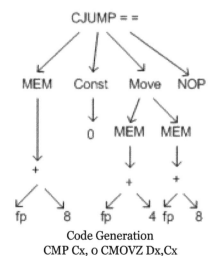

Code Generation

CMP Cx, 0 CMOVZ Dx,Cx

There is a clear intermediate code optimization - with 2 different sets of codes having 2 different parse trees. The optimized code does away with the redundancy in the original code and produces the same result.

Compiler Structure

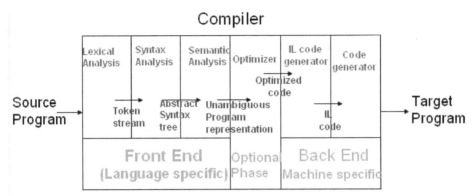

These are the various stages in the process of generation of the target code from the source code by the compiler. These stages can be broadly classified into

- the Front End (Language specific), and

- the Back End (Machine specific)parts of compilation.

- Information required about the program variables during compilation

  - Class of variable: keyword, identifier etc.

  - Type of variable: integer, float, array, function etc.

  - Amount of storage required

  - Address in the memory

  - Scope information

- Location to store this information

  - Attributes with the variable (has obvious problems)

  - At a central repository and every phase refers to the repository whenever information is required

- Normally the second approach is preferred

  - Use a data structure called symbol table

For the lexicons, additional information with its name may be needed. Information about whether it is a keyword/identifier, its data type, value, scope, etc might be needed to be known during the latter phases of compilation. However, all this information is not available in a straight away. This information has to be found and stored somewhere. We store it in a data structure called Symbol

Table. Thus each phase of the compiler can access data from the symbol table & write data to it. The method of retrieval of data is that with each lexicon a symbol table entry is associated. A pointer to this symbol in the table can be used to retrieve more information about the lexicon

Final Compiler Structure

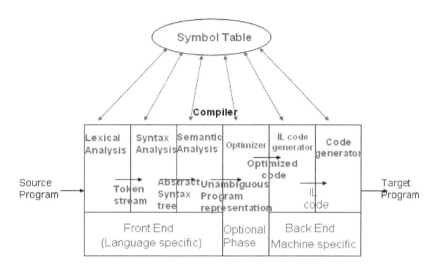

This diagram elaborates what's written. You can see that each stage can access the Symbol Table. All the relevant information about the variables, classes, functions etc. are stored in it.

Advantages of the Model

- Also known as Analysis-Synthesis model of compilation

    - Front end phases are known as analysis phases

    - Back end phases are known as synthesis phases

- Each phase has a well defined work

- Each phase handles a logical activity in the process of compilation

The Analysis-Synthesis model: The front end phases are Lexical, Syntax and Semantic analyses. These form the "analysis phase" as you can well see these all do some kind of analysis. The Back End phases are called the "synthesis phase" as they synthesize the intermediate and the target language and hence the program from the representation created by the Front End phases. The advantages are that not only can lots of code be reused, but also since the compiler is well structured - it is easy to maintain & debug.

- Compiler is retargetable

- Source and machine independent code optimization is possible.

- Optimization phase can be inserted after the front and back end phases have been developed and deployed

- Also known as Analysis-Synthesis model of compilation

Also since each phase handles a logically different phase of working of a compiler parts of the code can be reused to make new compilers. E.g., in a C compiler for Intel & Athlon the front ends will be similar. For a same language, lexical, syntax and semantic analyses are similar, code can be reused. Also in adding optimization, improving the performance of one phase should not affect the same of the other phase; this is possible to achieve in this model.

Issues in Compiler Design

- Compilation appears to be very simple, but there are many pitfalls

- How are erroneous programs handled?

- Design of programming languages has a big impact on the complexity of the compiler

- M*N vs. M+N problem

  - Compilers are required for all the languages and all the machines

  - For M languages and N machines we need to develop M*N compilers

  - However, there is lot of repetition of work because of similar activities in the front ends and back ends

  - Can we design only M front ends and N back ends, and some how link them to get all M*N compilers?

The compiler should fit in the integrated development environment. This opens many challenges in design e.g., appropriate information should be passed on to the debugger in case of erroneous programs. Also the compiler should find the erroneous line in the program and also make error recovery possible. Some features of programming languages make compiler design difficult, e.g., Algol68 is a very neat language with most good features. But it could never get implemented because of the complexities in its compiler design.

M*N vs M+N Problem

Universal Intermediate Language

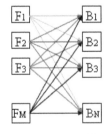
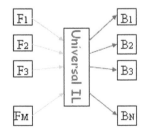

Requires M*N compilers   Requires M front ends
                                          And N back ends

We design the front end independent of machines and the back end independent of the source language. For this, we will require a Universal Intermediate Language (UIL) that acts as an interface between front end and back end. The front end will convert code written in the particular source language to the code in UIL, and the back end will convert the code in UIL to the equivalent code in the particular machine language. So, we need to design only M front ends and N back ends. To design a compiler for language L that produces output for machine C, we take the front end for L and the back end for C. In this way, we require only M + N compilers for M source languages and N machine architectures. For large M and N, this is a significant reduction in the effort.

Universal Intermediate Language

- Universal Computer/Compiler Oriented Language (UNCOL)

    - a vast demand for different compilers, as potentially one would require separate compilers for each combination of source language and target architecture. To counteract the anticipated combinatorial explosion, the idea of a linguistic switchbox materialized in 1958

    - UNCOL (UNiversal COmputer Language) is an intermediate language, which was proposed in 1958 to reduce the developmental effort of compiling many different languages to different architectures

Had there been no intermediate language then we would have needed a separate compiler for every combination of a source language and the target machine. This would have caused a combinatorial explosion as the number of languages or types of machines would have grown with time. Hence UNCOL was proposed to counteract this combinatorial explosion by acting as an intermediate language to reduce the effort of compiler development for different languages for different platforms.

    - The first intermediate language UNCOL (UNiversal Computer Oriented Language) was proposed in 1961 for use in compilers to reduce the development effort of compiling many different languages to many different architectures

    - the IR semantics should ideally be independent of both the source and target language (i.e. the target processor) Accordingly, already in the 1950s many researchers tried to define a single universal IR language, traditionally referred to as UNCOL (UNiversal Computer Oriented Language)

First suggested in 1958, its first version was proposed in 1961. The semantics of this language would be quite independent of the target language, and hence apt to be used as an Intermediate Language

    - it is next to impossible to design a single intermediate language to accommodate all programming languages

    - Mythical universal intermediate language sought since mid 1950s (Aho, Sethi, Ullman)

- However, common IRs for similar languages, and similar machines have been designed, and are used for compiler development

Due to vast differences between programming languages and machine architectures, design of such a language is not possible. But, we group programming languages with similar characteristics together and design an intermediate language for them. Similarly an intermediate language is designed for similar machines. The number of compilers though doesn't decrease to M + N, but is significantly reduced by use of such group languages.

How do we know Compilers Generate Correct Code?

- Prove that the compiler is correct.

- However, program proving techniques do not exist at a level where large and complex programs like compilers can be proven to be correct

- In practice do a systematic testing to increase confidence level

- Regression testing

  - Maintain a suite of test programs

  - Expected behavior of each program is documented

  - All the test programs are compiled using the compiler and deviations are reported to the compiler writer

- Design of test suite

  - Test programs should exercise every statement of the compiler at least once

  - Usually requires great ingenuity to design such a test suite

  - Exhaustive test suites have been constructed for some languages

Formal methods have been designed for automated testing of correctness of programs. But testing of very large programs like compilers, operating systems etc. is not possible by this method. These methods mainly rely on writing state of a program before and after the execution of a statement. The state consists of the values of the variables of a program at that step. In large programs like compilers, the number of variables is too large and so, defining the state is very difficult. So, formal testing of compilers has not yet been put to practice.

The solution is to go for systematic testing i.e., we will not prove that the compiler will work correctly in all situations but instead, we will test the compiler on different programs. Correct results increase the confidence that the compiler is correct.

Test suites generally contain 5000-10000 programs of various kinds and sizes. Such test suites are heavily priced as they are very intelligently designed to test every aspect of the compiler.

How to Reduce Development and Testing Effort?

- DO NOT WRITE COMPILERS

- GENERATE compilers

- A compiler generator should be able to "generate" compiler from the source language and target machine specifications

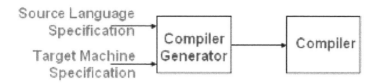

The compiler generator needs to be written only once. To generate any compiler for language L and generating code for machine M, we will need to give the compiler generator the specifications of L and M. This would greatly reduce effort of compiler writing as the compiler generator needs to be written only once and all compilers could be produced automatically.

Specifications and Compiler Generator

- How to write specifications of the source language and the target machine?
  - Language is broken into sub components like lexemes, structure, semantics etc.
  - Each component can be specified separately.

For example, an identifier may be specified as

- A string of characters that has at least one alphabet
- starts with an alphabet followed by alphanumeric
- letter (letter|digit)*
  - Similarly syntax and semantics can be described

Can target machine be described using specifications?

Tool based Compiler Development

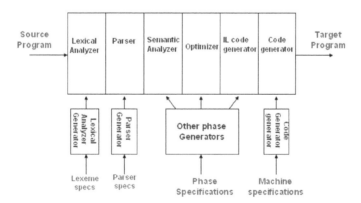

There are ways to break down the source code into different components like lexemes, structure, semantics etc. Each component can be specified separately. The above example shows the way of recognizing identifiers for lexical analysis. Similarly there are rules for semantic as well as syntax analysis. Can we have some specifications to describe the target machine?

Tools for each stage of compiler design have been designed that take in the specifications of the stage and output the compiler fragment of that stage. For example, lex is a popular tool for lexical analysis, yacc is a popular tool for syntactic analysis. Similarly, tools have been designed for each of these stages that take in specifications required for that phase e.g., the code generator tool takes in machine specifications and outputs the final compiler code. This design of having separate tools for each stage of compiler development has many advantages.

How to Retarget Compilers

- Changing specifications of a phase can lead to a new compiler

  - If machine specifications are changed then compiler can generate code for a different machine without changing any other phase

  - If front end specifications are changed then we can get compiler for a new language

- Tool based compiler development cuts down development/maintenance time by almost 30-40%

- Tool development/testing is one time effort

- Compiler performance can be improved by improving a tool and/or specification for a particular phase

In tool based compilers, change in one phase of the compiler doesn't affect other phases. Its phases are independent of each other and hence the cost of maintenance is cut down drastically. Just make a tool for once and then use it as many times as you want. With tools each time you need a compiler you won't have to write it, you can just "generate" it.

Bootstrapping

- Compiler is a complex program and should not be written in assembly language

- How to write compiler for a language in the same language (first time!)?

- First time this experiment was done for Lisp

- Initially, Lisp was used as a notation for writing functions.

- Functions were then hand translated into assembly language and executed

- McCarthy wrote a function eval[e,a] in Lisp that took a Lisp expression e as an argument

- The function was later hand translated and it became an interpreter for Lisp

Writing a compiler in assembly language directly can be a very tedious task. It is generally written in some high level language. What if the compiler is written in its intended source language itself ? This was done for the first time for Lisp. Initially, Lisp was used as a notation for writing functions. Functions were then hand translated into assembly language and executed. McCarthy wrote a function eval [e , a] in Lisp that took a Lisp expression e as an argument. Then it analyzed the expression and translated it into the assembly code. The function was later hand translated and it became an interpreter for Lisp.

- A compiler can be characterized by three languages: the source language (S), the target language (T), and the implementation language (I)

- The three language S, I, and T can be quite different. Such a compiler is called cross-compiler

- This is represented by a T-diagram as:

- In textual form this can be represented as:

$$S_I^T$$

Compilers are of two kinds: *native* and *cross* .

Native compilers are written in the same language as the target language. For example, SMM is a compiler for the language S that is in a language that runs on machine M and generates output code that runs on machine M.

Cross compilers are written in different language as the target language. For example, SNM is a compiler for the language S that is in a language that runs on machine N and generates output code that runs on machine M.

- Write a cross complier for a language L in implementation language S to generate code for machine N
- Existing compiler for S runs on a different machine M and generates code for M
- When Compiler LSN is run through SMM we get compiler LMN

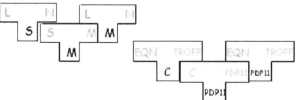

The compiler of LSN is written in language S. This compiler code is compiled once on SMM to generate the compiler's code in a language that runs on machine M. So, in effect, we get a compiler that converts code in language L to code that runs on machine N and the compiler itself is in language M. In other words, we get LMN.

- Suppose LLN is to be developed on a machine M where LMM is available

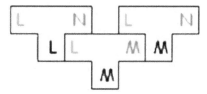

- Compile LLN second time using the generated compiler

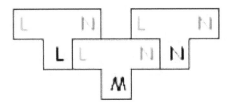

Using the technique described in the last slide, we try to use a compiler for a language L written in L. For this we require a compiler of L that runs on machine M and outputs code for machine M. First we write LLN i.e. we have a compiler written in L that converts code written in L to code that can run on machine N. We then compile this compiler program written in L on the available compiler LMM. So, we get a compiler program that can run on machine M and convert code written in L to code that can run on machine N i.e. we get LMN. Now, we again compile the original written compiler LLN on this new compiler LMN we got in last step. This compilation will convert the compiler code written in L to code that can run on machine N. So, we finally have a compiler code that can run on machine N and converts code in language L to code that will run on machine N. i.e. we get LNN.

Bootstrapping a Compiler: the Complete picture

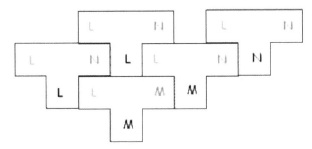

Bootstrapping is obtaining a compiler for a language L by writing the compiler code in the same language L.

Compilers of the 21 st Century

- Overall structure of almost all the compilers is similar to the structure we have discussed

- The proportions of the effort have changed since the early days of compilation

- Earlier front end phases were the most complex and expensive parts.

- Today back end phases and optimization dominate all other phases. Front end phases are typically a small fraction of the total time

Front end design has been almost mechanized now. Excellent tools have been designed that take in the syntactic structure and other specifications of the language and generate the front end automatically

References

- Cooper, Keith D., and Torczon, Linda, Engineering a Compiler, Morgan Kaufmann, 2004, ISBN 1-55860-699-8 page 404

- Peter van Eerten. "BaCon - A free BAsic CONverter for Unix, BSD and MacOSX". Basic-converter.org. Retrieved 2014-07-08

- "Java2c-transcompiler - A simple source-to-source from Java to C - Google Project Hosting". Retrieved 8 Oc-tober 2014

- Clinton F. Goss (August 2013) [First published June 1986]. "Machine Code Optimization - Improving Executable Object Code" (PDF) (Ph.D. dissertation). Computer Science Department Technical Report #246. Courant Institute, New York University. arXiv:1308.4815 . Retrieved 22 Aug 2013

- Cooper, Keith D.; Torczon, Linda (2003) [2002-01-01]. Engineering a Compiler. Morgan Kaufmann. pp. 404, 407. ISBN 978-1-55860-698-2

Lexical and Syntax Analysis

The major components of compiler design are discussed in this chapter. They are lexical, syntax and semantic analysis. The process of translating characters into identifiable tokens is called lexical analysis whereas in syntax analysis or parsing, the strings of symbols are examined keeping formal grammar as a base. After parsing, semantic code is collected. This is called semantic analysis.

Lexical Analysis

In computer science, lexical analysis is the process of converting a sequence of characters (such as in a computer program or web page) into a sequence of tokens (strings with an assigned and thus identified meaning). A program that performs lexical analysis may be termed a *lexer*, *tokenizer*, or *scanner*, though *scanner* is also a term for the first stage of a lexer. A lexer is generally combined with a parser, which together analyze the syntax of programming languages, web pages, and so forth.

Applications

A lexer forms the first phase of a compiler frontend in modern processing. Analysis generally occurs in one pass.

In older languages such as ALGOL, the initial stage was instead line reconstruction, which performed unstropping and removed whitespace and comments (and had scannerless parsers, with no separate lexer). These steps are now done as part of the lexer.

Lexers and parsers are most often used for compilers, but can be used for other computer language tools, such as prettyprinters or linters. Lexing can be divided into two stages: the *scanning*, which segments the input sequence into groups and categorizes these into token classes; and the *evaluating*, which converts the raw input characters into a processed value.

Lexers are generally quite simple, with most of the complexity deferred to the parser or semantic analysis phases, and can often be generated by a lexer generator, notably lex or derivatives. However, lexers can sometimes include some complexity, such as phrase structure processing to make input easier and simplify the parser, and may be written partly or fully by hand, either to support more features or for performance.

Lexeme

The word *lexeme* in computer science is defined differently than *lexeme* in linguistics. A lexeme in computer science roughly corresponds to what might be termed a word in linguistics (the term *word* in computer science has a different meaning than *word* in linguistics), although in some cases it may be more similar to a morpheme.

A *lexeme* is a string of characters which forms a syntactic unit.

Some authors term this a *token*, using 'token' interchangeably to represent (a) the string being tokenized, and (b) the token data structure resulting from putting this string through the tokenization process.

Token

A *token* or *lexical token* is a structure representing a lexeme that explicitly indicates its categorization for the purpose of parsing. A category of tokens is what might be termed a part-of-speech in linguistics. Examples of token categories may include *identifier* and *integer literal*, although the set of token categories differ in different programming languages. The process of forming tokens from an input stream of characters is called *tokenization*. Consider this expression in the programming language C:

sum= 3 + 2;

Tokenized and represented by the following table:

Lexeme	Token category
sum	Identifier
=	Assignment operator
3	Integer literal
+	Addition operator
2	Integer literal
;	End of statement

Lexical Grammar

The specification of a programming language often includes a set of rules, the lexical grammar, which defines the lexical syntax. The lexical syntax is usually a regular language, with the grammar rules consisting of regular expressions; they define the set of possible character sequences that are used to form individual tokens or lexemes. A lexer recognizes strings, and for each kind of string found the lexical program takes an action, most simply producing a token.

Two important common lexical categories are white space and comments. These are also defined in the grammar and processed by the lexer, but may be discarded (not producing any tokens) and considered *non-significant*, at most separating two tokens (as in if x instead of ifx). There are two important exceptions to this. First, in off-side rule languages that delimit blocks with indenting, initial whitespace is significant, as it determines block structure, and is generally handled at the lexer level; see phrase structure, below. Secondly, in some uses of lexers, comments and whitespace must be preserved – for examples, a prettyprinter also needs to output the comments and some debugging tools may provide messages to the programmer showing the original source code. In the 1960s, notably for ALGOL, whitespace and comments were eliminated as part of the line reconstruction phase (the initial phase of the compiler frontend), but this separate phase has been eliminated and these are now handled by the lexer.

Tokenization

Tokenization is the process of demarcating and possibly classifying sections of a string of input characters. The resulting tokens are then passed on to some other form of processing. The process can be considered a sub-task of parsing input.

Tokenization in the field of computer security has a different meaning.

For example, in the text string:

```
The quick brown fox jumps over the lazy dog
```

the string isn't implicitly segmented on spaces, as a natural language speaker would do. The raw input, the 43 characters, must be explicitly split into the 9 tokens with a given space delimiter (i.e., matching the string " " or regular expression /\s{1}/).

The tokens could be represented in XML,

```
<sentence>
   <word>The</word>
   <word>quick</word>
   <word>brown</word>
   <word>fox</word>
   <word>jumps</word>
   <word>over</word>
   <word>the</word>
   <word>lazy</word>
   <word>dog</word>
</sentence>
```

Or an s-expression,

```
(sentence
   (word The)
   (word quick)
   (word brown)
   (word fox)
   (word jumps)
   (word over)
   (word the)
```

```
(word lazy)

(word dog))
```

When a token class represents more than one possible lexeme, the lexer often saves enough information to reproduce the original lexeme, so that it can be used in semantic analysis. The parser typically retrieves this information from the lexer and stores it in the abstract syntax tree. This is necessary in order to avoid information loss in the case of numbers and identifiers.

Tokens are identified based on the specific rules of the lexer. Some methods used to identify tokens include: regular expressions, specific sequences of characters termed a flag, specific separating characters called delimiters, and explicit definition by a dictionary. Special characters, including punctuation characters, are commonly used by lexers to identify tokens because of their natural use in written and programming languages.

Tokens are often categorized by character content or by context within the data stream. Categories are defined by the rules of the lexer. Categories often involve grammar elements of the language used in the data stream. Programming languages often categorize tokens as identifiers, operators, grouping symbols, or by data type. Written languages commonly categorize tokens as nouns, verbs, adjectives, or punctuation. Categories are used for post-processing of the tokens either by the parser or by other functions in the program.

A lexical analyzer generally does nothing with combinations of tokens, a task left for a parser. For example, a typical lexical analyzer recognizes parentheses as tokens, but does nothing to ensure that each "(" is matched with a ")".

When a lexer feeds tokens to the parser, the representation used is typically an enumerated list of number representations. For example, "Identifier" is represented with 0, "Assignment operator" with 1, "Addition operator" with 2, etc.

Tokens are defined often by regular expressions, which are understood by a lexical analyzer generator such as lex. The lexical analyzer (generated automatically by a tool like lex, or hand-crafted) reads in a stream of characters, identifies the lexemes in the stream, and categorizes them into tokens. This is termed *tokenizing*. If the lexer finds an invalid token, it will report an error.

Following tokenizing is parsing. From there, the interpreted data may be loaded into data structures for general use, interpretation, or compiling.

Scanner

The first stage, the *scanner*, is usually based on a finite-state machine (FSM). It has encoded within it information on the possible sequences of characters that can be contained within any of the tokens it handles (individual instances of these character sequences are termed lexemes). For example, an *integer* token may contain any sequence of numerical digit characters. In many cases, the first non-whitespace character can be used to deduce the kind of token that follows and subsequent input characters are then processed one at a time until reaching a character that is not in the set of characters acceptable for that token (this is termed the *maximal munch*, or *longest match*, rule). In some languages, the lexeme creation rules are more complex and may involve backtracking over previously read characters. For example, in

C, one 'L' character is not enough to distinguish between an identifier that begins with 'L' and a wide-character string literal.

Evaluator

A lexeme, however, is only a string of characters known to be of a certain kind (e.g., a string literal, a sequence of letters). In order to construct a token, the lexical analyzer needs a second stage, the *evaluator*, which goes over the characters of the lexeme to produce a *value*. The lexeme's type combined with its value is what properly constitutes a token, which can be given to a parser. Some tokens such as parentheses do not really have values, and so the evaluator function for these can return nothing: only the type is needed. Similarly, sometimes evaluators can suppress a lexeme entirely, concealing it from the parser, which is useful for whitespace and comments. The evaluators for identifiers are usually simple (literally representing the identifier), but may include some unstropping. The evaluators for integer literals may pass the string on (deferring evaluation to the semantic analysis phase), or may perform evaluation themselves, which can be involved for different bases or floating point numbers. For a simple quoted string literal, the evaluator needs to remove only the quotes, but the evaluator for an escaped string literal incorporates a lexer, which unescapes the escape sequences.

For example, in the source code of a computer program, the string

```
net_worth_future= (assets - liabilities);
```

might be converted into the following lexical token stream; whitespace is suppressed and special characters have no value:

```
NAME net_worth_future

EQUALS

OPEN_PARENTHESIS

NAME assets

MINUS

NAME liabilities

CLOSE_PARENTHESIS

SEMICOLON
```

Though it is possible and sometimes necessary, due to licensing restrictions of existing parsers or if the list of tokens is small, to write a lexer by hand, lexers are often generated by automated tools. These tools generally accept regular expressions that describe the tokens allowed in the input stream. Each regular expression is associated with a production rule in the lexical grammar of the programming language that evaluates the lexemes matching the regular expression. These tools may generate source code that can be compiled and executed or construct a state transition table for a finite-state machine (which is plugged into template code for compiling and executing).

Regular expressions compactly represent patterns that the characters in lexemes might follow. For example, for an English-based language, a NAME token might be any English alphabetic character or an underscore, followed by any number of instances of ASCII alphanumeric characters and/or underscores. This could be represented compactly by the string `[a-zA-Z_][a-zA-Z_0-9]*`. This means "any character a-z, A-Z or _, followed by 0 or more of a-z, A-Z, _ or 0-9".

Regular expressions and the finite-state machines they generate are not powerful enough to handle recursive patterns, such as "n opening parentheses, followed by a statement, followed by n closing parentheses." They are unable to keep count, and verify that n is the same on both sides, unless a finite set of permissible values exists for n. It takes a full parser to recognize such patterns in their full generality. A parser can push parentheses on a stack and then try to pop them off and see if the stack is empty at the end.

The Lex tool and its compiler is designed to generate code for fast lexical analysers based on a formal description of the lexical syntax. It is generally considered insufficient for applications with a complex set of lexical rules and severe performance requirements. For example, the GNU Compiler Collection (GCC) uses hand-written lexers.

Lexer Generator

Lexers are often generated by a *lexer generator*, analogous to parser generators, and such tools often come together. The most established is lex, paired with the yacc parser generator, and the free equivalents flex/bison. These generators are a form of domain-specific language, taking in a lexical specification – generally regular expressions with some markup – and emitting a lexer.

These tools yield very fast development, which is very important in early development, both to get a working lexer and because a language specification may change often. Further, they often provide advanced features, such as pre- and post-conditions which are hard to program by hand. However, an automatically generated lexer may lack flexibility, and thus may require some manual modification, or an all-manually written lexer.

Lexer performance is a concern, and optimizing is worthwhile, more so in stable languages where the lexer is run very often (such as C or HTML). lex/flex-generated lexers are reasonably fast, but improvements of two to three times are possible using more tuned generators. Hand-written lexers are sometimes used, but modern lexer generators produce faster lexers than most hand-coded ones. The lex/flex family of generators uses a table-driven approach which is much less efficient than the directly coded approach. With the latter approach the generator produces an engine that directly jumps to follow-up states via goto statements. Tools like re2c have proven to produce engines that are between two and three times faster than flex produced engines. It is in general difficult to hand-write analyzers that perform better than engines generated by these latter tools.

List of Lexer Generators

- ANTLR – can generate lexical analyzers and parsers

- DFASTAR – generates DFA matrix table-driven lexers in C++

- Flex – variant of the classic *lex* for C/C++

- Ragel – state machine and lexer generator with output in C, C++, C#, Objective-C, D, Java, Go, and Ruby

- re2c – lexer generator for C and C++

The following lexical analysers can handle Unicode:

- JavaCC – generates lexical analyzers written in Java

- JFLex – lexical analyzer generator for Java.

- Quex – fast universal lexical analyzer generator for C and C++

- FsLex – lexer generator for byte and Unicode character input for F#

Phrase Structure

Lexical analysis mainly segments the input stream of characters into tokens, simply grouping the characters into pieces and categorizing them. However, the lexing may be significantly more complex; most simply, lexers may omit tokens or insert added tokens. Omitting tokens, notably whitespace and comments, is very common, when these are not needed by the compiler. Less commonly, added tokens may be inserted. This is done mainly to group tokens into statements, or statements into blocks, to simplify the parser.

Line Continuation

Line continuation is a feature of some languages where a newline is normally a statement terminator. Most often, ending a line with a backslash (immediately followed by a newline) results in the line being *continued* – the following line is *joined* to the prior line. This is generally done in the lexer: the backslash and newline are discarded, rather than the newline being tokenized. Examples include bash, other shell scripts and Python.

Semicolon Insertion

Many languages use the semicolon as a statement terminator. Most often this is mandatory, but in some languages the semicolon is optional in many contexts. This is mainly done at the lexer level, where the lexer outputs a semicolon into the token stream, despite one not being present in the input character stream, and is termed *semicolon insertion* or *automatic semicolon insertion*. In these cases, semicolons are part of the formal phrase grammar of the language, but may not be found in input text, as they can be inserted by the lexer. Optional semicolons or other terminators or separators are also sometimes handled at the parser level, notably in the case of trailing commas or semicolons.

Semicolon insertion is a feature of BCPL and its distant descendent Go, though it is absent in B or C. Semicolon insertion is present in JavaScript, though the rules are somewhat complex and much-criticized; to avoid bugs, some recommend always using semicolons, while others use initial semicolons, termed defensive semicolons, at the start of potentially ambiguous statements.

Semicolon insertion (in languages with semicolon-terminated statements) and line continuation (in languages with newline-terminated statements) can be seen as complementary: semicolon insertion adds a token, even though newlines generally do *not* generate tokens, while line continuation prevents a token from being generated, even though newlines generally *do* generate tokens.

Off-side Rule

The off-side rule (blocks determined by indenting) can be implemented in the lexer, as in Python, where increasing the indenting results in the lexer emitting an INDENT token, and decreasing the indenting results in the lexer emitting a DEDENT token. These tokens correspond to the opening brace { and closing brace } in languages that use braces for blocks, and means that the phrase grammar does not depend on whether braces or indenting are used. This requires that the lexer hold state, namely the current indent level, and thus can detect changes in indenting when this changes, and thus the lexical grammar is not context-free: INDENT–DEDENT depend on the contextual information of prior indent level.

Context-sensitive Lexing

Generally lexical grammars are context-free, or almost so, and thus require no looking back or ahead, or backtracking, which allows a simple, clean, and efficient implementation. This also allows simple one-way communication from lexer to parser, without needing any information flowing back to the lexer.

There are exceptions, however. Simple examples include: semicolon insertion in Go, which requires looking back one token; concatenation of consecutive string literals in Python, which requires holding one token in a buffer before emitting it and the off-side rule in Python, which requires maintaining a count of indent level (indeed, a stack of each indent level). These examples all only require lexical context, and while they complicate a lexer somewhat, they are invisible to the parser and later phases.

A more complex example is the lexer hack in C, where the token class of a sequence of characters cannot be determined until the semantic analysis phase, since typedef names and variable names are lexically identical but constitute different token classes. Thus in the hack, the lexer calls the semantic analyzer (say, symbol table) and checks if the sequence requires a typedef name. In this case, information must flow back not from the parser only, but from the semantic analyzer back to the lexer, which complicates design.

Lexical Grammar

In computer science, a lexical grammar is a formal grammar defining the syntax of tokens. The program is written using characters that are defined by the lexical structure of the language used. The character set is equivalent to the alphabet used by any written language. The lexical grammar lays down the rules governing how a character sequence is divided up into subsequences of characters, each part of which represents an individual token. This is frequently defined in terms of regular expressions.

For instance, the lexical grammar for many programming languages specifies that a string literal starts with a " character and continues until a matching " is found (escaping makes this more complicated), that an identifier is an alphanumeric sequence (letters and digits, usually also allowing underscores, and disallowing initial digits), and that an integer literal is a sequence of digits. So in the following character sequence "abc" xyz1 23 the tokens are *string*, *identifier* and *number* (plus whitespace tokens) because the space character terminates the sequence of characters forming the identifier. Further, certain sequences are categorized as keywords – these generally have the same form as identifiers (usually alphabetical words), but are categorized separately; formally they have a different token type.

Examples

Regular expressions for common lexical rules follow (for example, C).

Unescaped string literal (quote, followed by non-quotes, ending in a quote):

```
"[^"]*"
```

Escaped string literal (quote, followed sequence of escaped characters or non-quotes, ending in a quote):

```
"(\.|[^\"])*"
```

Integer literal:

```
[0-9]+
```

Decimal integer integer (no leading zero):

```
[1-9][0-9]*|0
```

Hexadecimal integer literal:

```
0[Xx][0-9A-Fa-f]+
```

Octal integer literal:

```
0[0-7]*
```

Identifier:

```
[A-Za-z_][A-Za-z0-9_]*
```

S-expression

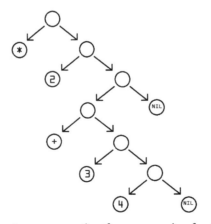

Tree data structure representing the s-expression for (* 2 (+ 3 4))

In computing, s-expressions, sexprs or sexps (for "symbolic expression") are a notation for nested list (tree-structured) data, invented for and popularized by the programming language Lisp, which uses them for source code as well as data. In the usual parenthesized syntax of Lisp, an s-expression is classically defined as

1. an atom, or

2. an expression of the form $(x \cdot y)$ where x and y are s-expressions.

The second, recursive part of the definition represents an ordered pair so that s-exprs are effectively binary trees.

The definition of an atom varies per context; in the original definition by John McCarthy, it was assumed that there existed "an infinite set of distinguishable atomic symbols" represented as "strings of capital Latin letters and digits with single embedded blanks" (i.e., character string and numeric literals). Most modern sexpr notations in addition use an abbreviated notation to represent lists in s-expressions, so that

```
(x y z)
```

stands for

```
(x . (y . (z . NIL)))
```

where `NIL` is the special end-of-list object (alternatively written (), which is the only representation in Scheme).

In the Lisp family of programming languages, s-expressions are used to represent both source code and data. Other uses of S-expressions are in Lisp-derived languages such as DSSSL, and as mark-up in communications protocols like IMAP and John McCarthy's CBCL. The details of the syntax and supported data types vary in the different languages, but the most common feature among these languages is the use of S-expressions and prefix notation.

Datatypes and Syntax

There are many variants of the S-expression format, supporting a variety of different syntaxes for different datatypes. The most widely supported are:

*   *Lists and pairs*: `(1 () (2 . 3) (4))`
*   *Symbols*: `with-hyphen ?@!$ a\ symbol\ with\ spaces`
*   *Strings*: `"Hello, world!"`
*   *Integers*: `-9876543210`
*   *Floating-point numbers*: `-0.0 6.28318 6.023e23`

The character # is often used to prefix extensions to the syntax, e.g. #x10 for hexadecimal integers, or #\C for characters.

Use in Lisp

When representing source code in Lisp, the first element of an S-expression is commonly an operator or function name and any remaining elements are treated as arguments. This is called "prefix notation" or "Polish notation". As an example, the Boolean expression written `4 == (2 + 2)` in C is represented as `(= 4 (+ 2 2))` in Lisp's s-expr-based prefix notation.

As noted above, the precise definition of "atom" varies across LISP-like languages. A quoted string can typically contain anything but a quote, while an unquoted identifier atom can typically contain anything but quote, whitespace characters, parenthesis, brackets, braces, backslash, and semicolon. In either case, a prohibited character can typically be included by escaping it with a preceding backslash. Unicode support varies.

The recursive case of the s-expr definition is traditionally implemented using cons cells.

S-expressions were originally intended only for data to be manipulated by M-expressions, but the first implementation of Lisp was an interpreter of S-expression encodings of M-expressions, and Lisp programmers soon became accustomed to using S-expressions for both code and data. This means that Lisp is homoiconic, that is, the primary representation of programs is also a data structure in a primitive type of the language itself.

Examples of Data S-expressions

Nested lists can be written as S-expressions: `((milk juice) (honey marmalade))` is a two-element S-expression whose elements are also two-element S-expressions. The whitespace-separated notation used in Lisp is typical. Line breaks (newline characters) usually qualify as separators.

This is a simple context-free grammar for a tiny subset of English written as an s-expression (Gazdar/Melish, Natural Language Processing in Lisp):

```
(((S) (NP VP))

 ((VP) (V))

 ((VP) (V NP))

 ((V) died)

 ((V) employed)

 ((NP) nurses)

 ((NP) patients)

 ((NP) Medicenter)

 ((NP) "Dr Chan"))
```

Example of Source Code S-expressions

Program code can be written in S-expressions, usually using prefix notation.

Example in Common Lisp:

```
(defun factorial (x)

   (if (zerop x)

      1

      (* x (factorial (- x 1)))))
```

S-expressions can be read in Lisp using the function READ. READ reads the textual representation of an s-expression and returns Lisp data. The function PRINT can be used to output an s-expression. The output then can be read with the function READ, when all printed data objects have a readable representation. Lisp has readable representations for numbers, strings, symbols, lists and many other data types. Program code can be formatted as pretty printed S-expressions using the function PPRINT (note: with two Ps, short for *pretty*-print).

Lisp programs are valid s-expressions, but not all s-expressions are valid Lisp programs. (1.0 + 3.1) is a valid s-expression, but not a valid Lisp program, since Lisp uses prefix notation and a floating point number (here 1.0) is not valid as an operation (the first element of the expression).

An S-expression preceded by a single quotation mark, as in 'x, is syntactic sugar for a quoted S-expression, in this case (quote x).

Parsing

S-Expressions are often compared to XML, a key difference being that S-Expressions are far simpler in syntax, therefore being much easier to parse. For instance, one could implement a simple S-Expression parser in just a few dozen lines of Python code.

```python
def parse_sexp(string):
    """

    >>> parse_sexp("(+ 5 (+ 3 5))")
    [['+', '5', ['+', '3', '5']]]


    """
    sexp = [[]]
    word = ''
    in_str = False
    for char in string:
        if char == '(' and not in_str:
            sexp.append([])
        elif char == ')' and not in_str:
            if word:
                sexp[-1].append(word)
                word = ''
            temp = sexp.pop()
            sexp[-1].append(temp)
        elif char in (' ', '\n', '\t') and not in_str:
            if word:
                sexp[-1].append(word)
```

```
            word = '/
        elif char == '\"':
            in_str = not in_str
        else:
            word += char
    return sexp
```

Standardization

Standards for some Lisp-derived programming languages include a specification for their S-expression syntax. These include Common Lisp (ANSI standard document ANSI INCITS 226-1994 (R2004)), Scheme (R5RS and R6RS), and ISLISP.

Rivest's Variant

In May 1997, Ron Rivest submitted an Internet-Draft to be considered for publication as an RFC. The draft defined a syntax based on Lisp S-expressions but intended for general-purpose data storage and exchange (similar to XML) rather than specifically for programming. It was never approved as an RFC, but it has since been cited and used by other RFCs (e.g. RFC 2693) and several other publications. It was originally intended for use in SPKI.

Rivest's format defines an S-expression as being either an octet-string (a series of bytes) or a finite list of other S-expressions. It describes three interchange formats for expressing this structure. One is the "advanced transport", which is very flexible in terms of formatting, and is syntactically similar to Lisp-style expressions, but they are not identical. The advanced transport, for example, allows octet-strings to be represented verbatim (the string's length followed by a colon and the entire raw string), a quoted form allowing escape characters, hexadecimal, Base64, or placed directly as a "token" if it meets certain conditions. (Rivest's tokens differ from Lisp tokens in that the former are just for convenience and aesthetics, and treated exactly like other strings, while the latter have specific syntactical meaning.)

Rivest's draft defines a canonical representation "for digital signature purposes". It's intended to be compact, easier to parse, and unique for any abstract S-expression. It only allows verbatim strings, and prohibits whitespace as formatting outside strings. Finally there is the "basic transport representation", which is either the canonical form or the same encoded as Base64 and surrounded by braces, the latter intended to safely transport a canonically encoded S-expression in a system which might change spacing (e.g. an email system which has 80-character-wide lines and wraps anything longer than that).

This format has not been widely adapted for use outside of SPKI. Rivest's S-expressions web page provides C source code for a parser and generator (available under the MIT license), which could be adapted and embedded into other programs. In addition, there are no restrictions on independently implementing the format.

Abstract Syntax Tree

In computer science, an abstract syntax tree (AST), or just syntax tree, is a tree representation of the abstract syntactic structure of source code written in a programming language. Each node of the tree denotes a construct occurring in the source code. The syntax is "abstract" in not representing every detail appearing in the real syntax. For instance, grouping parentheses are implicit in the tree structure, and a syntactic construct like an if-condition-then expression may be denoted by means of a single node with three branches.

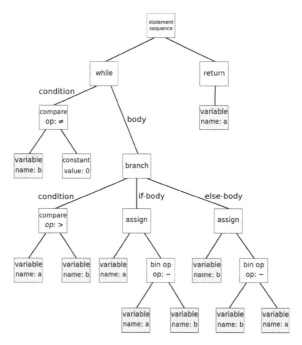

An abstract syntax tree for the following code for the Euclidean algorithm:

```
while b ≠ 0
if a > b
a := a - b
else
b := b - a
return a
```

This distinguishes abstract syntax trees from concrete syntax trees, traditionally designated parse trees, which are often built by a parser during the source code translation and compiling process. Once built, additional information is added to the AST by means of subsequent processing, e.g., contextual analysis.

Abstract syntax trees are also used in program analysis and program transformation systems.

Application in Compilers

Abstract syntax trees are data structures widely used in compilers, due to their property of representing the structure of program code. An AST is usually the result of the syntax analysis phase of a compiler. It often serves as an intermediate representation of the program through several stages that the compiler requires, and has a strong impact on the final output of the compiler.

Motivation

Being the product of the syntax analysis phase of a compiler, the AST has several properties that are invaluable to the further steps of the compilation process.

- Compared to the source code, an AST does not include certain elements, such as inessential punctuation and delimiters (braces, semicolons, parentheses, etc.).

- A more important difference is that the AST can be edited and enhanced with information such as properties and annotations for every element it contains. Such editing and annotation is impossible with the source code of a program, since it would imply changing it.

- At the same time, an AST usually contains extra information about the program, due to the consecutive stages of analysis by the compiler, an example being the position of an element in the source code. This information may be used to notify the user of the location of an error in the code.

ASTs are needed because of the inherent nature of programming languages and their documentation. Languages are often ambiguous by nature. In order to avoid this ambiguity, programming languages are often specified as a context-free grammar (CFG). However, there are often aspects of programming languages that a CFG can't express, but are part of the language and are documented in its specification. These are details that require a context to determine their validity and behaviour. For example, if a language allows new types to be declared, a CFG cannot predict the names of such types nor the way in which they should be used. Even if a language has a predefined set of types, enforcing proper usage usually requires some context. Another example is duck typing, where the type of an element can change depending on context. Operator overloading is yet another case where correct usage and final function are determined based on the context. Java provides an excellent example, where the '+' operator is both numerical addition and concatenation of strings.

Although there are other data structures involved in the inner workings of a compiler, the AST performs a unique function. During the first stage, the syntax analysis stage, a compiler produces a parse tree. This parse tree can be used to perform almost all functions of a compiler by means of syntax-directed translation. Although this method can lead to a more efficient compiler, it goes against the software engineering principles of writing and maintaining programs. Another advantage that the AST has over a parse tree is the size, particularly the smaller height of the AST and the smaller number of elements.

Design

The design of an AST is often closely linked with the design of a compiler and its expected features.

Core requirements include the following:

- Variable types must be preserved, as well as the location of each declaration in source code.

- The order of executable statements must be explicitly represented and well defined.

- Left and right components of binary operations must be stored and correctly identified.

- Identifiers and their assigned values must be stored for assignment statements.

These requirements can be used to design the data structure for the AST.

Some operations will always require two elements, such as the two terms for addition. However, some language constructs require an arbitrarily large number of children, such as argument lists passed to programs from the command shell. As a result, an AST used to represent code written in such a language has to also be flexible enough to allow for quick addition of an unknown quantity of children.

Another major design requirement for an AST is that it should be possible to unparse an AST into source code form. The source code produced should be sufficiently similar to the original in appearance and identical in execution, upon recompilation.

Design Patterns

Due to the complexity of the requirements for an AST and the overall complexity of a compiler, it is beneficial to apply sound software development principles. One of these is to use proven design patterns to enhance modularity and ease of development.

Different operations don't necessarily have different types, so it is important to have a sound node class hierarchy. This is crucial in the creation and the modification of the AST as the compiler progresses.

Because the compiler traverses the tree several times to determine syntactic correctness, it is important to make traversing the tree a simple operation. The compiler executes a specific set of operations, depending on the type of each node, upon reaching it, so it often makes sense to use the visitor pattern.

Usage

The AST is used intensively during semantic analysis, where the compiler checks for correct usage of the elements of the program and the language. The compiler also generates symbol tables based on the AST during semantic analysis. A complete traversal of the tree allows verification of the correctness of the program.

After verifying correctness, the AST serves as the base for code generation. The AST is often used to generate the 'intermediate representation' '(IR)', sometimes called an intermediate language, for the code generation.

Unified AST

Since an AST is written specifically for a single programming language, program analysis and program transformation systems written against the AST are also specific to a single programming language. However, programming languages from the same family often share similar syntactic constructs. Thus it should be possible to write program analysis and program transformation systems in a language agnostic fashion using a unified AST. A unified AST is a tree representation of the abstract syntactic structure of source code written in several programming language.

- Recognize tokens and ignore white spaces, comments

i	f		(	×	1		*	×	2	<	1	.	0	)	{

Generates token stream

if	(	×1	*	×2	<	1.0	)	{

- Error reporting

- Model using regular expressions

- Recognize using Finite State Automata

The first phase of the compiler is lexical analysis. The lexical analyzer breaks a sentence into a sequence of words or tokens and ignores white spaces and comments. It generates a stream of tokens from the input. This is modeled through regular expressions and the structure is recognized through finite state automata. If the token is not valid i.e., does not fall into any of the identifiable groups, then the lexical analyzer reports an error. Lexical analysis thus involves recognizing the tokens in the source program and reporting errors, if any. We will study more about all these processes in the subsequent slides.

- Sentences consist of string of tokens (a syntactic category) for example, number, identifier, keyword, string

- Sequences of characters in a token is a lexeme for example, 100.01, counter, const, "How are you?"

- Rule of description is a pattern for example, letter(letter/digit)*

- Discard whatever does not contribute to parsing like white spaces (blanks, tabs, newlines) and comments

- construct constants: convert numbers to token num and pass number as its attribute, for example, integer 31 becomes <num, 31>

- recognize keyword and identifiers for example counter = counter + increment becomes id = id + id /*check if id is a keyword*/

We often use the terms "token", "pattern" and "lexeme" while studying lexical analysis. Lets see what each term stands for.

Token: A token is a syntactic category. Sentences consist of a string of tokens. For example number, identifier, keyword, string etc are tokens.

Lexeme: Sequence of characters in a token is a lexeme. For example 100.01, counter, const, "How are you?" etc are lexemes.

Pattern: Rule of description is a pattern. For example letter (letter | digit)* is a pattern to symbolize a set of strings which consist of a letter followed by a letter or digit. In general, there is a set of strings in the input for which the same token is produced as output. This set of strings is described by a rule called a *pattern* associated with the token. This pattern is said to *match* each string in the set. A *lexeme* is a sequence of characters in the source program that is matched by the pattern for a token. The patterns are specified using regular expressions. For example, in the Pascal statement

Const pi = 3.1416;

The substring pi is a lexeme for the token "identifier". We discard whatever does not contribute to parsing like white spaces (blanks, tabs, new lines) and comments. When more than one pattern matches a lexeme, the lexical analyzer must provide additional information about the particular lexeme that matched to the subsequent phases of the compiler. For example, the pattern num matches both 1 and 0 but it is essential for the code generator to know what string was actually matched. The lexical analyzer collects information about tokens into their associated attributes. For example integer 31 becomes <num, 31>. So, the constants are constructed by converting numbers to token ‹num› and passing the number as its attribute. Similarly, we recognize keywords and identifiers. For example count = count + inc becomes id = id + id.

Interface to Other Phases

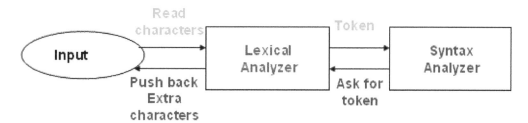

- Push back is required due to lookahead for example > = and >

- It is implemented through a buffer

  - Keep input in a buffer

  - Move pointers over the input

The lexical analyzer reads characters from the input and passes tokens to the syntax analyzer whenever it asks for one. For many source languages, there are occasions when the lexical analyzer needs to look ahead several characters beyond the current lexeme for a pattern before a match can be announced. For example, > and >= cannot be distinguished merely on the basis of the first character >. Hence there is a need to maintain a buffer of the input for look ahead and push back. We keep the input in a buffer and move pointers over the input. Sometimes, we may also need to push back extra characters due to this lookahead character.

Approaches to Implementation

- Use assembly language Most efficient but most difficult to implement

- Use high level languages like C Efficient but difficult to implement

- Use tools like lex, flex Easy to implement but not as efficient as the first two cases

Lexical analyzers can be implemented using many approaches/techniques:

- Assembly language: We have to take input and read it character by character. So we need to have control over low level I/O. Assembly language is the best option for that because it is the most efficient. This implementation produces very efficient lexical analyzers. However, it is most difficult to implement, debug and maintain.

- High level language like C: Here we will have a reasonable control over I/O because of high-level constructs. This approach is efficient but still difficult to implement.

- Tools like Lexical Generators and Parsers: This approach is very easy to implement, only specifications of the lexical analyzer or parser need to be written. The lex tool produces the corresponding C code. But this approach is not very efficient which can sometimes be an issue. We can also use a hybrid approach wherein we use high level languages or efficient tools to produce the basic code and if there are some hot-spots (some functions are a bottleneck) then they can be replaced by fast and efficient assembly language routines.

Construct a Lexical Analyzer

- Allow white spaces, numbers and arithmetic operators in an expression

- Return tokens and attributes to the syntax analyzer

- A global variable tokenval is set to the value of the number

- Design requires that

    - A finite set of tokens be defined

    - Describe strings belonging to each token

We now try to construct a lexical analyzer for a language in which white spaces, numbers and arithmetic operators in an expression are allowed. From the input stream, the lexical analyzer recognizes the tokens and their corresponding attributes and returns them to the syntax analyzer. To achieve this, the function returns the corresponding token for the lexeme and sets a global variable, say tokenval , to the value of that token. Thus, we must define a finite set of tokens and specify the strings belonging to each token. We must also keep a count of the line number for the purposes of reporting errors and debugging. We will have a look at a typical code snippet which implements a lexical analyzer in the subsequent slide.

```
#include <stdio.h>

#include <ctype.h>

int lineno = 1;

int tokenval = NONE;

int lex() {

        int t;

        while (1) {
```

```
            t = getchar ();

            if (t = = ‹ ‹ || t = = ‹\t›);

            else if (t = = ‹\n›)lineno = lineno + 1;

            else if (isdigit (t) ) {

        tokenval = t - ‹0› ;

        t = getchar ();

        while (isdigit(t)) {

    tokenval = tokenval * 10 + t - ‹0› ;

    t = getchar();

}

ungetc(t,stdin);

return num;

}

else { tokenval = NONE;return t; }

}

}
```

A crude implementation of lex() analyzer to eliminate white space and collect numbers is shown. Every time the body of the while statement is executed, a character is read into t. If the character is a blank (written ' ') or a tab (written '\t'), then no token is returned to the parser; we merely go around the while loop again. If a character is a new line (written '\n'), then a global variable "lineno" is incremented, thereby keeping track of line numbers in the input, but again no token is returned. Supplying a line number with the error messages helps pin point errors. The code for reading a sequence of digits is on lines 11-19. The predicate isdigit(t) from the include file <ctype.h> is used on lines 11 and 14 to determine if an incoming character t is a digit. If it is, then its integer value is given by the expression t-'0' in both ASCII and EBCDIC. With other character sets, the conversion may need to be done differently.

Problems

- Scans text character by character

- Look ahead character determines what kind of token to read and when the current token ends

- First character cannot determine what kind of token we are going to read

The problem with lexical analyzer is that the input is scanned character by character. Now, its not possible to determine by only looking at the first character what kind of token we are going to read since it might be common in multiple tokens. We saw one such an example of > and >= previously. So one needs to use a lookahead character depending on which one can determine what kind of token to read or when does a particular token end. It may not be a punctuation or a blank but just another kind of token which acts as the word boundary. The lexical analyzer that we just saw used a function ungetc() to push lookahead characters back into the input stream. Because a large amount of time can be consumed moving characters, there is actually a lot of overhead in processing an input character. To reduce the amount of such overhead involved, many specialized buffering schemes have been developed and used.

Symbol Table

- Stores information for subsequent phases

- Interface to the symbol table

    - Insert(s,t): save lexeme s and token t and return pointer

    - Lookup(s): return index of entry for lexeme s or 0 if s is not found

Implementation of symbol table

- Fixed amount of space to store lexemes. Not advisable as it waste space.

- Store lexemes in a separate array. Each lexeme is separated by eos. Symbol table has pointers to lexemes.

A data structure called symbol table is generally used to store information about various source language constructs. Lexical analyzer stores information in the symbol table for the subsequent phases of the compilation process. The symbol table routines are concerned primarily with saving and retrieving lexemes. When a lexeme is saved, we also save the token associated with the lexeme. As an interface to the symbol table, we have two functions

    - Insert(s , t): Saves and returns index of new entry for string s , token t .

    - Lookup(s): Returns index of the entry for string s , or 0 if s is not found.

Next, we come to the issue of implementing a symbol table. The symbol table access should not be slow and so the data structure used for storing it should be efficient. However, having a fixed amount of space to store lexemes is not advisable because a fixed amount of space may not be large enough to hold a very long identifier and may be wastefully large for a short identifier, such as i . An alternative is to store lexemes in a separate array. Each lexeme is terminated by an end-of-string, denoted by EOS, that may not appear in identifiers. The symbol table has pointers to these lexemes.

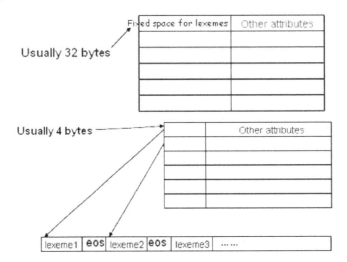

Here, we have shown the two methods of implementing the symbol table. As, we can see, the first one which is based on allotting fixed amount space for each lexeme tends to waste a lot of space by using a fixed amount of space for each lexeme even though that lexeme might not require the whole of 32 bytes of fixed space. The second representation which stores pointers to a separate array, which stores lexemes terminated by an EOS, is a better space saving implementation. Although each lexeme now has an additional overhead of five bytes (four bytes for the pointer and one byte for the EOS). Even then we are saving about 70% of the space which we were wasting in the earlier implementation. We allocate extra space for 'Other Attributes' which are filled in the later phases.

How to Handle Keywords?

- Consider token DIV and MOD with lexemes div and mod.

- Initialize symbol table with insert("div" , DIV) and insert("mod" , MOD).

- Any subsequent lookup returns a nonzero value, therefore, cannot be used as an identifier .

To handle keywords, we consider the keywords themselves as lexemes. We store all the entries corresponding to keywords in the symbol table while initializing it and do lookup whenever we see a new lexeme. Now, whenever a lookup is done, if a nonzero value is returned, it means that there already exists a corresponding entry in the Symbol Table. So, if someone tries to use a keyword as an identifier, it will not be allowed as an identifier with this name already exists in the Symbol Table. For instance, consider the tokens *DIV* and *MOD* with lexemes "div" and "mod". We initialize symbol table with insert("div", DIV) and insert("mod", MOD). Any subsequent lookup now would return a nonzero value, and therefore, neither "div" nor "mod" can be used as an identifier.

Difficulties in Design of Lexical Analyzers

- Is it as simple as it sounds?

- Lexemes in a fixed position. Fix format vs. free format languages

- Handling of blanks

  - in Pascal, blanks separate identifiers

  - in Fortran, blanks are important only in literal strings for example variable counter is same as count er

  - Another example

  DO 10 I = 1.25   DO10I=1.25

  DO 10 I = 1,25   DO10I=1,25

The design of a lexical analyzer is quite complicated and not as simple as it looks. There are several kinds of problems because of all the different types of languages we have. Let us have a look at some of them. For example: 1. We have both fixed format and free format languages - A lexeme is a sequence of character in source program that is matched by pattern for a token. FORTRAN has lexemes in a fixed position. These white space and fixed format rules came into force due to punch cards and errors in punching. Fixed format languages make life difficult because in this case we have to look at the position of the tokens also. 2. Handling of blanks - It's of our concern that how do we handle blanks as many languages (like Pascal, FORTRAN etc) have significance for blanks and void spaces. When more than one pattern matches a lexeme, the lexical analyzer must provide additional information about the particular lexeme that matched to the subsequent phases of the lexical analyzer. In Pascal blanks separate identifiers. In FORTRAN blanks are important only in literal strings. For example, the variable " counter " is same as " count er ".

Another example is DO 10 I = 1.25 DO 10 I = 1,25 The first line is a variable assignment DO10I = 1.25. The second line is the beginning of a Do loop. In such a case we might need an arbitrary long lookahead. Reading from left to right, we cannot distinguish between the two until the " , " or " . " is reached.

- The first line is a variable assignment

DO10I=1.25

- second line is beginning of a

Do loop

- Reading from left to right one can not distinguish between the two until the ";" or "." is reached

- • Fortran white space and fixed format rules came into force due to punch cards and errors in punching

In the example,

DO 10 I = 1.25   DO 10 I = 1,25

The first line is a variable assignment DO10I = 1.25. The second line is the beginning of a Do loop. In such a case, we might need an arbitrary long lookahead. Reading from left to right, we can not distinguish between the two until the " , " or " . " is reached.

FORTRAN has a language convention which impacts the difficulty of lexical analysis. The alignment of lexeme may be important in determining the correctness of the source program; the treatment of blank varies from language to language such as FORTRAN and ALGOL 68. Blanks are not significant except in little strings. The conventions regarding blanks can greatly complicate the task of identified tokens.

Punched Cards (raw).

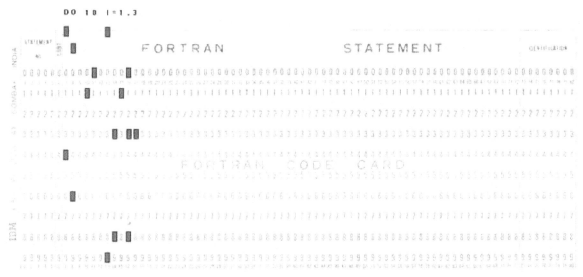

Punched Cards (punched).

PL/1 Problems

- Keywords are not reserved in PL/1 if then then then = else else else = then if if then then = then + 1

- PL/1 declarations

Declare(arg 1 ,arg 2 ,arg 3 ,...,arg n)

- Cannot tell whether Declare is a keyword or array reference until after ") "

- Requires arbitrary lookahead and very large buffers . Worse, the buffers may have to be reloaded.

In many languages certain strings are reserved, i.e., there meaning is predefined and cannot be changed by the user. If keywords are not reserved then the lexical analyzer must distinguish between a keyword and a user defined identifier. PL/1 has several problems: 1. In PL/1 keywords are not reserved; thus, the rules for distinguishing keywords from identifiers are quite complicated as the following PL/1 statement illustrates. For example - If then then then = else else else = then 2. PL/1 declarations: Example - Declare (arg1, arg2, arg3,.., argn) In this statement, we can not tell whether 'Declare' is a keyword or array name until we see the character that follows the ")". This requires arbitrary lookahead and very large buffers. This buffering scheme works quite well most of the time but with it the amount of lookahead is limited and this limited lookahead may make it impossible to recognize tokens in salutations where the distance the forward pointer must travel is more than the length of the buffer, as the slide illustrates. The situation even worsens if the buffers have to be reloaded.

Problem Continues Even Today!!

- C++ template syntax:Foo<Bar>

- C++ stream syntax: cin >> var;

- Nested templates: Foo<Bar<Bazz>>

- Can these problems be resolved by lexical analyzers alone?

Even C++ has such problems like:

1. C++ template syntax: Foo<Bar>

2. C++ stream syntax: cin >> var;

3. Nested templates: Foo<Bar<Bazz>>

We have to see if these problems be resolved by lexical analyzers alone.

How to Specify Tokens?

- How to describe tokens

2.e0 20.e-01 2.000

- How to break text into token

if (x==0) a = x << 1;

iff (x==0) a = x < 1;

- How to break input into token efficiently

    - Tokens may have similar prefixes

    - Each character should be looked at only once

The various issues which concern the specification of tokens are:

1. How to describe the complicated tokens like e0 20.e-01 2.000

2. How to break into tokens the input statements like if (x==0) a = x << 1; iff (x==0) a = x < 1;

3. How to break the input into tokens efficiently?There are the following problems that are encountered:

    - Tokens may have similar prefixes

    - Each character should be looked at only once

How to Describe Tokens?

- Programming language tokens can be described by regular languages

- Regular languages

    - Are easy to understand

    - There is a well understood and useful theory

    - They have efficient implementation

- Regular languages have been discussed in great detail in the "Theory of Computation" course

Here we address the problem of describing tokens. Regular expression is an important notation for specifying patterns. Each pattern matches a set of strings, so regular expressions will serve as names for set of strings. Programming language tokens can be described by regular languages. The specification of regular expressions is an example of an recursive definition. Regular languages are easy to understand and have efficient implementation. The theory of regular languages is well understood and very useful. There are a number of algebraic laws that are obeyed by regular expression which can be used to manipulate regular expressions into equivalent forms.

Operations on Languages

- L U M = {s | s is in L or s is in M}

- LM = {st | s is in L and t is in M}

- $L^* = $ Union of L^i such that $0 \leq i \leq \infty$

where $L^0 = \in$ and $L^i = L^{i-1} L$

The various operations on languages are:

- Union of two languages L and M written as L U M = {s | s is in L or s is in M}

- Concatenation of two languages L and M written as LM = {st | s is in L and t is in M}

- The Kleene Closure of a language L written as

- $L^* = $ Union of L^i such that $0 \leq i \leq \infty$ where $L^0 = \in$ and $L^i = L^{i-1} L$

We will look at various examples of these operators in the subsequent slide.

Example

- Let L = {a, b, .., z} and D = {0, 1, 2, . 9} then

- LUD is a set of letters and digits

- LD is a set of strings consisting of a letter followed by a digit

- L* is a set of all strings of letters including ?

- L(LUD)* is a set of all strings of letters and digits beginning with a letter

- D + is a set of strings of one or more digits

Example:

Let L be a the set of alphabets defined as L = {a, b, .., z} and D be a set of all digits defined as D = {0, 1, 2, .., 9}. We can think of L and D in two ways. We can think of L as an alphabet consisting of the set of lower case letters, and D as the alphabet consisting of the set the ten decimal digits.

Alternatively, since a symbol can be regarded as a string of length one, the sets L and D are each finite languages. Here are some examples of new languages created from L and D by applying the operators defined.

- Union of L and D, L U D is the set of letters and digits.

- Concatenation of L and D, LD is the set of strings consisting of a letter followed by a digit.

- The Kleene closure of L, L* is a set of all strings of letters including ? .

- L(LUD)* is the set of all strings of letters and digits beginning with a letter.

- D+ is the set of strings one or more digits.

Notation

- Let S be a set of characters. A language over S is a set of strings of characters belonging to S

- A regular expression r denotes a language L(r)

- Rules that define the regular expressions over S

  - ? is a regular expression that denotes { ? } the set containing the empty string

  - If a is a symbol in S then a is a regular expression that denotes {a}

Let S be a set of characters. A language over S is a set of strings of characters belonging to S . A regular expression is built up out of simpler regular expressions using a set of defining rules. Each regular expression r denotes a language L(r). The defining rules specify how L(r) is formed by combining in various ways the languages denoted by the sub expressions of r . Following are the rules that define the regular expressions over S :

- ? is a regular expression that denotes { ? }, that is, the set containing the empty string.

- If a is a symbol in S then a is a regular expression that denotes { a } i.e., the set containing the string a . Although we use the same notation for all three, technically, the regular expression a is different from the string a or the symbol a . It will be clear from the context whether we are talking about a as a regular expression, string or symbol.

- If r and s are regular expressions denoting the languages L(r) and L(s) then

- (r)|(s) is a regular expression denoting L(r) U L(s)

- (r)(s) is a regular expression denoting L(r)L(s)

- (r)* is a regular expression denoting (L(r))*

- (r) is a regular expression denoting L(r)

Suppose r and s are regular expressions denoting the languages L(r) and L(s). Then,

- (r)|(s) is a regular expression denoting L(r) U L(s).

- (r) (s) is a regular expression denoting L(r) L(s).

- (r)* is a regular expression denoting (L(r))*.

- (r) is a regular expression denoting L(r).

Let us take an example to illustrate: Let S = {a, b}.

1. The regular expression a|b denotes the set {a,b}.

2. The regular expression (a | b) (a | b) denotes {aa, ab, ba, bb}, the set of all strings of a's and b's of length two. Another regular expression for this same set is aa | ab | ba | bb.

3. The regular expression a* denotes the set of all strings of zero or more a's i.e., { ? , a, aa, aaa, .}.

4. The regular expression (a | b)* denotes the set of all strings containing zero or more instances of an a or b, that is, the set of strings of a's and b's. Another regular expression for this set is (a*b*)*.

5. The regular expression a | a*b denotes the set containing the string a and all strings consisting of zero or more a's followed by a b.

If two regular expressions contain the same language, we say r and s are equivalent and write r = s. For example, (a | b) = (b | a).

- Precedence and associativity

- *, concatenation, and | are left associative

- * has the highest precedence

- Concatenation has the second highest precedence

- | has the lowest precedence

Unnecessary parentheses can be avoided in regular expressions if we adopt the conventions that:

- The unary operator * has the highest precedence and is left associative.

- Concatenation has the second highest precedence and is left associative.

- | has the lowest precedence and is left associative. Under these conventions, (a)|((b)*(c)) is equivalent to a|b*c. Both expressions denote the set of strings that are either a single a or zero or more b 's followed by one c .

How to Specify Tokens

Reguler Definitions

Let r_i be a regular expression and d_i be a distinct name

Regular definition is a sequence of definitions of the form

$d_1 \rightarrow r_1$

$d_2 \rightarrow r_2$

......

$d_n \rightarrow r_n$

Where each r_i is a regular expression over $\Sigma \cup \{d_1, d_2, ..., d_{i-1}\}$

If S is an alphabet of basic symbols, then a regular definition is a sequence of definitions of the form

$d_1 \rightarrow r_1$

$d_2 \rightarrow r_2$

....

$d_n \rightarrow r_n$

where each di is a distinct name, and each ri is a regular expression over the symbols in $\sum \cup \{d_1, d_2, ..., d_{i-1}\}$ i.e. the basic symbols and the previously defined names. By restricting each ri to symbols of S and the previously defined names, we can construct a regular expression over S for any ri by repeatedly replacing regular-expression names by the expressions they denote. If ri used dkfor some k >= i, then ri might be recursively defined, and this substitution process would not terminate. So, we treat tokens as terminal symbols in the grammar for the source language. The lexeme matched by the pattern for the token consists of a string of characters in the source program and can be treated as a lexical unit. The lexical analyzer collects information about tokens into there associated attributes. As a practical matter a token has usually only a single attribute, appointed to the symbol table entry in which the information about the token is kept; the pointer becomes the attribute for the token.

Examples

- My Fax number
  $91 - (512) - 259 - 7586$
- $\Sigma = \text{digits} \cup \{-,(,)\}$
- Country $\rightarrow$ digit$^+$ digit^2
- Area $\rightarrow$ $'('$digit$^+$$')'$ digit^3
- Exchange $\rightarrow$ digit$^+$ digit^3
- Phone $\rightarrow$ digit$^+$ digit^4
- Number $\rightarrow$ country $'-'$ area $'-'$ exchange $'-'$ phone

As an example, let us consider a fax number 91-(512)-259-7586.

The regular definitions for writing any fax number will be:

Set of alphabets being S $= \text{digits} \cup \{-,(,)\}$

Country $\rightarrow$ digit$^+$ $\qquad$ $\left(\text{digit}^2\right)$ i.e. a string of two digits.

Area $\rightarrow$ $'\left('\text{digit}^+'\right)'$ $\qquad$ $\left(\text{digit}^3\right)$ i.e. a string of three digits.

Exchange $\rightarrow$ digit$^+$ $\qquad$ $\left(\text{digit}^3\right)$ i.e. a string of three digits.

Phone $\rightarrow$ digit$^+$ $\qquad$ $\left(\text{digit}^4\right)$ i.e. a string of four digits.

Number $\rightarrow$ country '−' area '−' exchange '−' phone

In this case we also need to define the number of digits in each token.

Examples

- My email address ska@iitk.ac.in
- S = letter U {@, . }
- Letter $\longrightarrow$ a| b| .| z| A| B| .| Z
- Name $\longrightarrow$ letter +
- Address $\longrightarrow$ name ‹@› name '.' name '.' name

Now we look at the regular definitions for writing an email address ska@iitk.ac.in:

Set of alphabets being S = letter U {@, . }):

Letter $\longrightarrow$ a| b| .| z| A| B| .| Z i.e., any lower case or upper case alphabet

Name $\longrightarrow$ letter + i.e., a string of one or more letters

Address $\longrightarrow$ name ‹@› name '.' name '.' name

Examples

. Identifier

letter $\longrightarrow$ a| b| .|z| A| B| .| Z

digit $\longrightarrow$ 0| 1| .| 9

identifier $\longrightarrow$ letter(letter|digit)*

. Unsigned number in Pascal

digit $\longrightarrow$ 0| 1| . |9

digits $\longrightarrow$ digit +

fraction $\longrightarrow$ ' . ' digits | ε

exponent $\longrightarrow$ (E (' + ' | ' - ' |ε) digits) | ε

number $\longrightarrow$ digits fraction exponent

Here are some more examples:

The set of Identifiers is the set of strings of letters and digits beginning with a letter. Here is a regular definition for this set:

letter $\longrightarrow$ a| b| .|z| A| B| .| Z i.e., any lower case or upper case alphabet

digit $\longrightarrow$ 0| 1| .| 9 i.e., a single digit

identifier $\longrightarrow$ letter(letter | digit)* i.e., a string of letters and digits beginning with a letter

Unsigned numbers in Pascal are strings such as 5280, 39.37, 6.336E4, 1.894E-4. Here is a regular definition for this set:

digit $\longrightarrow$ 0| 1| .|9 i.e., a single digit

digits $\longrightarrow$ digit + i.e., a string of one or more digits

fraction $\longrightarrow$ '.' digits | ε i.e., an empty string or a decimal symbol followed by one or more digits

exponent $\longrightarrow$ (E ('+' | '-' | ε) digits) | ε

number $\longrightarrow$ digits fraction exponent

Regular Expressions in Specifications

- Regular expressions describe many useful languages
- Regular expressions are only specifications; implementation is still required
- Given a string s and a regular expression R, does s ? L(R) ?
- Solution to this problem is the basis of the lexical analyzers
- However, just the yes/no answer is not important
- Goal: Partition the input into tokens

Regular expressions describe many useful languages. A regular expression is built out of simpler regular expressions using a set of defining rules. Each regular expression R denotes a regular language L(R). The defining rules specify how L(R) is formed by combining in various phases the languages denoted by the sub expressions of R. But regular expressions are only specifications, the implementation is still required. The problem before us is that given a string s and a regular expression R , we have to find whether s e L(R). Solution to this problem is the basis of the lexical analyzers. However, just determining whether s e L(R) is not enough. In fact, the goal is to partition the input into tokens. Apart from this we have to do bookkeeping and push back the extra characters.

1. Write a regular expression for lexemes of each token

- number $\rightarrow$ digit^{+}
- identifier $\rightarrow$ letter(letter digit)$^{+}$

2. Construct R matching all lexemes of all tokens

- $R = R1 + R2 + R3 + ...$

3. Let input be $X_1.....X_n$

- $for 1 \leq i \leq n\, check X_1.....X_i \, \varepsilon\, L(R)$

4. $X_1.....X_i \, \varepsilon\, L(R) \Rightarrow X_1.....X_i \, \varepsilon\, L(Ri) for some j$

- Smallest such j is token class of $X_1.....X_i$

5. Remove $X_1.....X_i$ from input; go to (3)

For notational convenience, we may wish to give names to regular expressions and to define regular expressions using these names as if they were symbols. The algorithm for breaking input into tokens is as follows:

1. Write a regular expression for lexemes of each token. For example,

number   digit $^+$; Regular expression representing a

                                         string of one or more digits

identifier   letter (letter I digit)$^+$; Regular expression representing a string

                                         starting with a letter

                                        ; Followed by a letter or digit

2. Construct a regular expression R matching all lexemes of all tokens given by

$$R = R1 + R2 + R3 + ...$$

3. Let input be $x_1...x_i$
   for $1 \leq i \leq n$
      check $x_1...x_i \, \varepsilon\, L(R)$

4. If $x_1...x_i \, \varepsilon\, L(R)$ then $x_1...x_i \, \varepsilon\, L(R)$ for some j

   Smallest such j is token class of $x_1...x_i$

5. Remove $x_1...x_i$ from the input and again reiterate through Step 3 onwards

- The algorithm gives priority to tokens listed earlier

   - Treats "if" as keyword and not identifier

- How much input is used? What if

   - $x_1 .x_i$? L(R)

   - $x_1.x_j$? L(R)

   - Pick up the longest possible string in L(R)

- The principle of "maximal munch"

- Regular expressions provide a concise and useful notation for string patterns

- Good algorithms require a single pass over the input

A simple technique for separating keywords and identifiers is to initialize appropriately the symbol table in which information about identifier is saved. The algorithm gives priority to the tokens listed earlier and hence treats "if" as keyword and not identifier. The technique of placing keywords in the symbol table is almost essential if the lexical analyzer is coded by hand. Without doing so the number of states in a lexical analyzer for a typical programming language is several hundred, while using the trick, fewer than a hundred states would suffice. If a token belongs to more than one category, then we go by priority rules such as " first match " or " longest match ". So we have to prioritize our rules to remove ambiguity. If both $x1 .xi$ and $x1 .xj \varepsilon L(R)$ then we pick up the longest possible string in $L(R)$. This is the principle of " maximal munch ". Regular expressions provide a concise and useful notation for string patterns. Our goal is to construct a lexical analyzer that will isolate the lexeme for the next token in the input buffer and produce as output a pair consisting of the appropriate token and attribute value using the translation table. We try to use a algorithm such that we are able to tokenize our data in single pass. Basically we try to efficiently and correctly tokenize the input data.

How to Break up Text

Elsex=0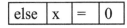

- Regular expressions alone are not enough

- Normally longest match wins

- Ties are resolved by prioritizing tokens

- Lexical definitions consist of regular definitions, priority rules and maximal munch principle

We can see that regular expressions are not sufficient to help us in breaking up our text. Let us consider the example " elsex=0 ".In different programming languages this might mean " else x=0 " or "elsex=0". So the regular expressions alone are not enough. In case there are multiple possibilities, normally the longest match wins and further ties are resolved by prioritizing tokens. Hence lexical definitions consist of regular definitions, priority rules and prioritizing principles like maximal munch principle. The information about the language that is not in the regular language of the tokens can be used to pinpoint the errors in the input. There are several ways in which the redundant matching in the transitions diagrams can be avoided.

Finite Automata

- Regular expression are declarative specifications

- Finite automata is an implementation

- A finite automata consists of

- An input alphabet belonging to S

- A set of states S

- A set of transitions statei⟶ statej

- A set of final states F

- A start state n

- Transition s1 ⟶ s2 is read:

in state s1 on input a go to state s2

- If end of input is reached in a final state then accept

A recognizer for language is a program that takes as input a string x and answers yes if x is the sentence of the language and no otherwise. We compile a regular expression into a recognizer by constructing a generalized transition diagram called a finite automaton. Regular expressions are declarative specifications and finite automaton is the implementation. It can be deterministic or non deterministic, both are capable of recognizing precisely the regular sets. Mathematical model of finite automata consists of:

- An input alphabet belonging to S - The set of input symbols,

- A set of states S ,

- A set of transitions statei ⟶statej , i.e., a transition function move that maps states symbol pairs to the set of states,

- A set of final states F or accepting states, and

- A start state n . If end of input is reached in a final state then we accept the string, otherwise reject it.

- Otherwise, reject

Pictorial Notation

- A state

- A final state

- Transition

- Transition from state i to state j on an input a

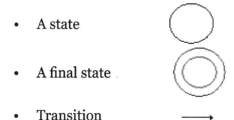
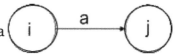

A state is represented by a circle, a final state by two concentric circles and a transition by an arrow.

How to Recognize Tokens

- Consider

relop ⟶ < | <= | = | <> | >= | >

id ⟶ letter(letter|digit)*

num ⟶ digit + ('.' digit +)? (E('+'|'-')? digit +)?

delim ⟶ blank | tab | newline

ws ⟶ delim +

- Construct an analyzer that will return <token, attribute> pairs

We now consider the following grammar and try to construct an analyzer that will return <token, attribute> pairs.

relop ⟶ < | = | = | <> | = | >

id ⟶ letter (letter | digit)*

num ⟶ digit+ ('.' digit+) ? (E ('+' | '-')? digit+)?

delim ⟶ blank | tab | newline

ws ⟶ delim+

Using set of rules as given in the example above we would be able to recognize the tokens. Given a regular expression R and input string x , we have two methods for determining whether x is in L(R). One approach is to use algorithm to construct an NFA N from R, and the other approach is using a DFA.

Transition Diagram for Relops

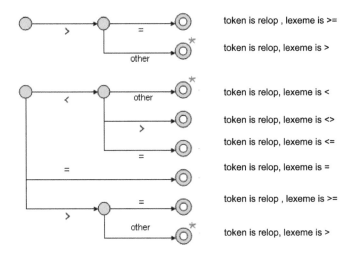

In case of < or >, we need a lookahead to see if it is a <, = , or <> or = or >. We also need a global data structure which stores all the characters. In lex, yylex is used for storing the lexeme. We can recognize the lexeme by using the transition diagram. Depending upon the number of checks a relational operator uses, we land up in a different kind of state like >= and > are different. From the transition diagram in the slide it's clear that we can land up into six kinds of relops.

Transition Diagram for Identifier

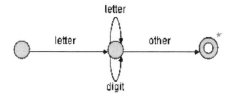

Transition Diagram for White Spaces

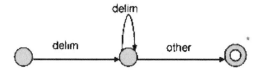

Transition diagram for identifier : In order to reach the final state, it must encounter a letter followed by one or more letters or digits and then some other symbol. Transition diagram for white spaces : In order to reach the final state, it must encounter a delimiter (tab, white space) followed by one or more delimiters and then some other symbol.

Transition Diagram for Unsigned Numbers

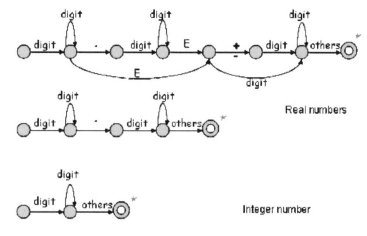

Transition diagram for Unsigned Numbers : We can have *three* kinds of unsigned numbers and hence need three transition diagrams which distinguish each of them. The first one recognizes *exponential* numbers. The second one recognizes *real* numbers. The third one recognizes *integers*

- The lexeme for a given token must be the longest possible

- Assume input to be 12.34E56

- Starting in the third diagram the accept state will be reached after 12

- Therefore, the matching should always start with the first transition diagram

- If failure occurs in one transition diagram then retract the forward pointer to the start state and activate the next diagram

- If failure occurs in all diagrams then a lexical error has occurred

The lexeme for a given token must be the longest possible. For example, let us assume the input to be 12.34E56 . In this case, the lexical analyzer must not stop after seeing 12 or even 12.3. If we start at the third diagram (which recognizes the integers), the accept state will be reached after 12. Therefore, the matching should always start with the first transition diagram. In case a failure occurs in one transition diagram then we retract the forward pointer to the start state and start analyzing using the next diagram. If failure occurs in all diagrams then a lexical error has occurred i.e. the input doesn't pass through any of the three transition diagrams. So we need to prioritize our rules and try the transition diagrams in a certain order (changing the order may put us into trouble). We also have to take care of the principle of maximal munch i.e. the automata should try matching the longest possible token as lexeme.

Implementation of Transition Diagrams

```
Token nexttoken() {
        while(1) {
                switch (state) {
    ..
        case 10 : c=nextchar();
        if(isletter(c)) state=10;
        elseif (isdigit(c)) state=10; else state=11;
        break;
        ..
        }
    }
}
```

Another Transition Diagram for Unsigned Numbers

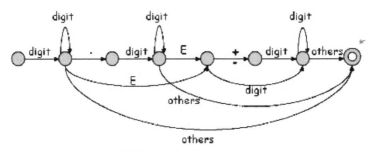

A more complex transition diagram is difficult to implement and may give rise to errors during coding, however, there are ways to better implementation

We can reduce the number of transition diagrams (automata) by clubbing all these diagrams into a single diagram in some cases. But because of two many arrows going out of each state the complexity of the code may increase very much. This may lead to creeping in of errors during coding. So it is not advisable to reduce the number of transition diagrams at the cost of making them too complex to understand. However, if we use multiple transition diagrams, then the tradeoff is that we may have to unget() a large number of characters as we need to recheck the entire input in some other transition diagram.

Lexical Analyzer Generator

- Input to the generator

  - List of regular expressions in priority order

  - Associated actions for each of regular expression (generates kind of token and other book keeping information)

- Output of the generator

  - Program that reads input character stream and breaks that into tokens

  - Reports lexical errors (unexpected characters), if any

We assume that we have a specification of lexical analyzers in the form of regular expression and the corresponding action parameters. Action parameter is the program segments that is to be executed whenever a lexeme matched by regular expressions is found in the input. So, the input to the generator is a list of regular expressions in a priority order and associated actions for each of the regular expressions. These actions generate the kind of token and other book keeping information. Our problem is to construct a recognizer that looks for lexemes in the input buffer. If more than one pattern matches, the recognizer is to choose the longest lexeme matched. If there are two or more patterns that match the longest lexeme, the first listed matching pattern is chosen. So, the output of the generator is a program that reads input character stream and breaks that into tokens. It also reports in case there is a lexical error i.e. either unexpected characters occur or an input string doesn›t match any of the regular expressions.

LEX: A Lexical Analyzer Generator

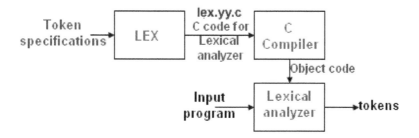

In this section, we consider the design of a software tool that automatically constructs the lexical analyzer code from the LEX specifications. LEX is one such lexical analyzer generator which produces C code based on the token specifications. This tool has been widely used to specify lexical analyzers for a variety of languages. We refer to the tool as Lex Compiler, and to its input specification as the Lex language. Lex is generally used in the manner depicted in the slide. First, a specification of a lexical analyzer is prepared by creating a program lex.l in the lex language. Then, the lex.l is run through the Lex compiler to produce a C program lex.yy.c . The program lex.yy.c consists of a tabular representation of a transition diagram constructed from the regular expressions of the lex.l, together with a standard routine that uses the table to recognize lexemes. The actions associated with the regular expressions in lex.l are pieces of C code and are carried over directly to lex.yy.c. Finally, lex.yy.c is run through the C compiler to produce an object program a.out which is the lexical analyzer that transforms the input stream into a sequence of tokens.

How does LEX Work?

- Regular expressions describe the languages that can be recognized by finite automata

- Translate each token regular expression into a non deterministic finite automaton (NFA)

- Convert the NFA into an equivalent DFA

- Minimize the DFA to reduce number of states

- Emit code driven by the DFA tables

In this section, we will describe the working of lexical analyzer tools such as LEX. LEX works on some fundamentals of regular expressions and NFA - DFA. First, it reads the regular expressions which describe the languages that can be recognized by finite automata. Each token regular expression is then translated into a corresponding non-deterministic finite automaton (NFA). The NFA is then converted into an equivalent deterministic finite automaton (DFA). The DFA is then minimized to reduce the number of states. Finally, the code driven by DFA tables is emitted.

Syntax Analysis

- Check syntax and construct abstract syntax tree

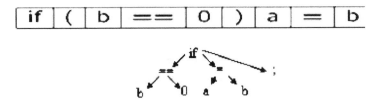

- Error reporting and recovery
- Model using context free grammars
- Recognize using Push down automata/Table Driven Parsers

This is the second phase of the compiler. In this phase, we check the syntax and construct the abstract syntax tree. This phase is modeled through context free grammars and the structure is recognized through push down automata or table-driven parsers. The syntax analysis phase verifies that the string can be generated by the grammar for the source language. In case of any syntax errors in the program, the parser tries to report as many errors as possible. Error reporting and recovery form a very important part of the syntax analyzer. The error handler in the parser has the following goals: . It should report the presence of errors clearly and accurately. . It should recover from each error quickly enough to be able to detect subsequent errors. . It should not significantly slow down the processing of correct programs.

What Syntax Analysis cannot do!

- To check whether variables are of types on which operations are allowed

- To check whether a variable has been declared before use

- To check whether a variable has been initialized

- These issues will be handled in semantic analysis

The information which syntax analysis phase gets from the previous phase (lexical analysis) is whether a token is valid or not and which class of tokens does it belong to. Hence it is beyond the capabilities of the syntax analysis phase to settle issues like:

- Whether or not a variable has already been declared?

- Whether or not a variable has been initialized before use?

- Whether or not a variable is of the type on which the operation is allowed?

All such issues are handled in the semantic analysis phase.

Limitations of Regular Languages

- How to describe language syntax precisely and conveniently. Can regular expressions be used?

- Many languages are not regular, for example, string of balanced parentheses

  - $((((.))))$

  - $\{ (i) i \mid i = 0 \}$

  - There is no regular expression for this language

- A finite automata may repeat states, however, it cannot remember the number of times it has been to a particular state

- A more powerful language is needed to describe a valid string of tokens

Regular expressions cannot be used to describe language syntax precisely and conveniently. There are many languages which are not regular. For example, consider a language consisting of all strings of balanced parentheses. There is no regular expression for this language. Regular expressions can not be used for syntax analysis (specification of grammar) because:. The pumping lemma for regular languages prevents the representation of constructs like a string of balanced parenthesis where there is no limit on the number of parenthesis. Such constructs are allowed by most of the programming languages.. This is because a finite automaton may repeat states, however, it does not have the power to remember the number of times a state has been reached.. Many programming languages have an inherently recursive structure that can be defined by Context Free Grammars (CFG) rather intuitively. So a more powerful language is needed to describe valid string of tokens.

Syntax Definition

- Context free grammars

    - a set of tokens (terminal symbols)

    - a set of non terminal symbols

    - a set of productions of the form nonterminal ⟶ String of terminals & non terminals

    - a start symbol <T, N, P, S>

- A grammar derives strings by beginning with a start symbol and repeatedly replacing a non terminal by the right hand side of a production for that non terminal.

- The strings that can be derived from the start symbol of a grammar G form the language L(G) defined by the grammar.

In this section, we review the definition of a context free grammar and introduce terminology for talking about parsing. A context free grammar has four components:

- A set of tokens , known as terminal symbols. Terminals are the basic symbols from which strings are formed.

- A set of non-terminals . Non-terminals are syntactic variables that denote sets of strings. The non-terminals define sets of strings that help define the language generated by the grammar.

- A set of productions . The productions of a grammar specify the manner in which the terminals and non-terminals can be combined to form strings. Each production consists of a non-terminal called the left side of the production, an arrow, and a sequence of tokens and/ or on- terminals, called the right side of the production.

- A designation of one of the non-terminals as the start symbol , and the set of strings it denotes is the language defined by the grammar.

The strings are derived from the start symbol by repeatedly replacing a non-terminal (initially the start symbol) by the right hand side of a production for that non-terminal.

Examples

- String of balanced parentheses

$S \longrightarrow (S) S \mid \varepsilon$

- Grammar

list $\longrightarrow$ list + digit | list - digit | digit

digit $\longrightarrow$ 0 | 1 | . | 9 Consists of the language which is a list of digit separated by + or -.

$S \longrightarrow (S) S \mid \varepsilon$

is the grammar for a string of balanced parentheses.

For example, consider the string: (( )( )). It can be derived as:

S (S)S $\longrightarrow$ ((S)S)S $\longrightarrow$ (( )S)S $\longrightarrow$ (( )(S)S)S $\longrightarrow$ (( )( )S)S $\longrightarrow$ (( )( ))S $\longrightarrow$ (( )( ))

Similarly,

list $\longrightarrow$ list + digit

| list - digit

| digit digit $\longrightarrow$ 0 | 1 | . | 9

is the grammar for a string of digits separated by + or -.

Derivation

list $\longrightarrow$ list + digit

      $\longrightarrow$ list - digit + digit

      $\longrightarrow$ digit - digit + digit

      $\longrightarrow$ 9 - digit + digit

      $\longrightarrow$ 9 - 5 + digit

      $\longrightarrow$ 9 - 5 + 2

Therefore, the string 9-5+2 belongs to the language specified by the grammar.

The name context free comes from the fact that use of a production $X \longrightarrow$. does not depend on the context of X

For example, consider the string 9 - 5 + 2 . It can be derived as:

list $\longrightarrow$ list + digit $\longrightarrow$ list - digit + digit $\longrightarrow$ digit - digit + digit $\longrightarrow$ 9 - digit + digit $\longrightarrow$ 9 - 5 + digit $\longrightarrow$ 9 - 5 + 2

It would be interesting to know that the name context free grammar comes from the fact that use of a production $X \longrightarrow$. does not depend on the context of X.

Examples .

- Grammar for Pascal block

block ⟶ begin statements end

statements ⟶ stmt-list | ε

stmt-list ⟶ stmt-list ; stmt

| stmt

block ⟶ begin statements end

statements ⟶ stmt-list | ε

stmt-list ⟶ stmt-list ; stmt

| stmt

is the grammar for a block of Pascal language.

Syntax Analyzers

- Testing for membership whether w belongs to L(G) is just a "yes" or "no" answer

- However the syntax analyzer

  - Must generate the parse tree

  - Handle errors gracefully if string is not in the language

- Form of the grammar is important

  - Many grammars generate the same language

  - Tools are sensitive to the grammar

A parse tree may be viewed as a graphical representation for a derivation that filters out the choice regarding replacement order. Each interior node of a parse tree is labeled by some non-terminal A , and that the children of the node are labeled, from left to right, by the symbols in the right side of the production by which this A was replaced in the derivation. A syntax analyzer not only tests whether a construct is syntactically correct i.e. belongs to the language represented by the specified grammar but also generates the parse tree. It also reports appropriate error messages in case the string is not in the language represented by the grammar specified. It is possible that many grammars represent the same language. However, the tools such as *yacc* or other parser generators are sensitive to the grammar form. For example, if the grammar has shift-shift or shift-reduce conflicts, the parser tool will give appropriate warning message. We will study about these in details in the subsequent sections.

Derivation

- If there is a production A ⟶ a then we say that A derives a and is denoted by A ⟹ a

- a A ß ⟹ a γ ß if A ⟶ γ is a production

- If a1 $\Rightarrow$ a2 $\Rightarrow$. $\Rightarrow$ an then a 1 $\Rightarrow$ an

- Given a grammar G and a string w of terminals in L(G) we can write S $\Rightarrow$ w

- If S $\Rightarrow$ a where a is a string of terminals and non terminals of G then we say that a is a sentential form of G

If there is a production A $\longrightarrow$ a then it is read as " A derives a " and is denoted by A $\Rightarrow$ a . The production tells us that we could replace one instance of an A in any string of grammar symbols by a .

In a more abstract setting, we say that a A ß $\Rightarrow$ a γ ß if A $\longrightarrow$? is a production and a and ß are arbitrary strings of grammar symbols

If a 1 $\Rightarrow$ a 2 $\Rightarrow$. $\Rightarrow$ a n then we say a 1 derives a n . The symbol $\Rightarrow$ means "derives in one step". Often we wish to say "derives in one or more steps". For this purpose, we can use the symbol $\Rightarrow$ with a + on its top. Thus, if a string w of terminals belongs to a grammar G, it

+   *

is written as S $\Rightarrow$ w . If S $\Rightarrow$ a , where a may contain non-terminals, then we say that a is a sentential form of G. A sentence is a sentential form with no non-terminals.

- If in a sentential form only the leftmost non terminal is replaced then it becomes leftmost derivation

- Every leftmost step can be written as wAγ $\Rightarrow$ lm* wδγ where w is a string of terminals and A $\longrightarrow$ δ is a production

- Similarly, right most derivation can be defined

- An ambiguous grammar is one that produces more than one leftmost/rightmost derivation of a sentence

Consider the derivations in which only the leftmost non-terminal in any sentential form is replaced at each step. Such derivations are termed leftmost derivations. If a $\Rightarrow$ ß by a step in which the leftmost non-terminal in a is replaced, we write a $\Rightarrow$ lm ß . Using our notational conventions, every leftmost step can be written wAγ $\Rightarrow$ lmwdγ where w consists of terminals only, A $\longrightarrow$ d is the production applied, and ? is a string of grammar symbols. If a derives ß by a leftmost derivation, then we write a $\Rightarrow$ lm* ß . If S $\Rightarrow$ lm* a , then we say a is a left-sentential form of the grammar at hand. Analogous definitions hold for rightmost derivations in which the rightmost non-terminal is replaced at each step. Rightmost derivations are sometimes called the canonical derivations. A grammar that produces more than one leftmost or more than one rightmost derivation for some sentence is said to be ambiguous . Put another way, an ambiguous grammar is one that produces more than one parse tree for some sentence is said to be ambiguous.

Parse Tree

- It shows how the start symbol of a grammar derives a string in the language

- root is labeled by the start symbol

- leaf nodes are labeled by tokens

- Each internal node is labeled by a non terminal

- if A is a non-terminal labeling an internal node and x_1, x_2, .x_n are labels of the children of that node then A⟶ $x_1 x_2$. x_n is a production

A parse tree may be viewed as a graphical representation for a derivation that filters out the choice regarding replacement order. Thus, a parse tree pictorially shows how the start symbol of a grammar derives a string in the language. Each interior node of a parse tree is labeled by some non-terminal A , and that the children of the node are labeled, from left to right, by the symbols in the right side of the production by which this A was replaced in the derivation. The root of the parse tree is labeled by the start symbol and the leaves by non-terminals or terminals and, read from left to right, they constitute a sentential form, called the yield or frontier of the tree. So, if A is a non-terminal labeling an internal node and x_1 , x_2 , .x_n are labels of children of that node then A ⟶ $x_1 x_2$. x_n is a production.

Example

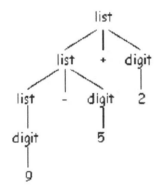

The parse tree for 9-5+2 implied by the derivation.

- 9 is a *list* by production (3), since 9 is a digit.

- 9-5 is a *list* by production (2), since 9 is a list and 5 is a digit.

- 9-5+2 is a *list* by production (1), since 9-5 is a list and 2 is a digit.

Production 1: list ⟶ list + digit

Production 2: list ⟶ list - digit

Production 3: list ⟶ digit

digit ⟶ 0|1|2|3|4|5|6|7|8|9

Ambiguity

- A Grammar can have more than one parse tree for a string

Consider grammar

string ⟶ string + string

| string - string

| 0 | 1 | . | 9

- String 9-5+2 has two parse trees

A grammar is said to be an ambiguous grammar if there is some string that it can generate in more than one way (i.e., the string has more than one parse tree or more than one leftmost derivation). A language is inherently ambiguous if it can only be generated by ambiguous grammars.

For example, consider the following grammar:

string ⟶ string + string

| string - string

| 0 | 1 | . | 9

In this grammar, the string 9-5+2 has two possible parse trees as shown below.

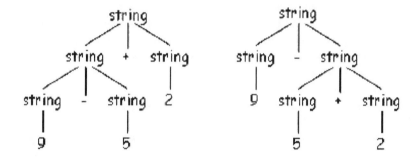

Consider the parse trees for string 9-5+2, expression like this has more than one parse tree. The two trees for 9-5+2 correspond to the two ways of parenthesizing the expression: (9-5)+2 and 9-(5+2). The second parenthesization gives the expression the value 2 instead of 6.

- Ambiguity is problematic because meaning of the programs can be incorrect
- Ambiguity can be handled in several ways
    - Enforce associativity and precedence
    - Rewrite the grammar (cleanest way)
- There are no general techniques for handling ambiguity
- It is impossible to convert automatically an ambiguous grammar to an unambiguous one

Ambiguity is harmful to the intent of the program. The input might be deciphered in a way which was not really the intention of the programmer, as shown above in the 9-5+2 example. Though there is no general technique to handle ambiguity i.e., it is not possible to develop some feature which automatically identifies and removes ambiguity from any grammar. However, it can be removed, broadly speaking, in the following possible ways:-

1) Rewriting the whole grammar unambiguously.

2) Implementing precedence and associatively rules in the grammar.

Associativity

- If an operand has operator on both the sides, the side on which operator takes this operand is the associativity of that operator

- In a+b+c b is taken by left +

- +, -, *, / are left associative

- ^, = are right associative

- Grammar to generate strings with right associative operators right à letter = right | letter letter ⟶ a| b |.| z

A binary operation * on a set S that does not satisfy the associative law is called non-associative. A left-associative operation is a non-associative operation that is conventionally evaluated from left to right i.e., operand is taken by the operator on the left side.

For example,

6*5*4 = (6*5)*4 and not 6*(5*4)

6/5/4 = (6/5)/4 and not 6/(5/4)

A right-associative operation is a non-associative operation that is conventionally evaluated from right to left i.e., operand is taken by the operator on the right side.

For example,

6^5^4 => 6^(5^4) and not (6^5)^4

x=y=z=5 => x=(y=(z=5))

Following is the grammar to generate strings with left associative operators. (Note that this is left recursive and may go into infinite loop. But we will handle this problem later on by making it right recursive)

left ⟶ left + letter | letter

letter ⟶ a | b | .... | z

Precedence

- String a+5*2 has two possible interpretations because of two different parse trees corresponding to

    (a+5)*2 and a+(5*2)

- Precedence determines the correct interpretation.

Precedence is a simple ordering, based on either importance or sequence. One thing is said to "take precedence" over another if it is either regarded as more important or is to be performed first. For example, consider the string a+5*2. It has two possible interpretations because of two different parse trees corresponding to (a+5)*2 and a+(5*2). But the * operator has precedence over the + operator. So, the second interpretation is correct. Hence, the precedence determines the correct interpretation.

Parsing

Parsing, syntax analysis or syntactic analysis is the process of analysing a string of symbols, either in natural language or in computer languages, conforming to the rules of a formal grammar. The term *parsing* comes from Latin *pars* (*orationis*), meaning part (of speech).

The term has slightly different meanings in different branches of linguistics and computer science. Traditional sentence parsing is often performed as a method of understanding the exact meaning of a sentence or word, sometimes with the aid of devices such as sentence diagrams. It usually emphasizes the importance of grammatical divisions such as subject and predicate.

Within computational linguistics the term is used to refer to the formal analysis by a computer of a sentence or other string of words into its constituents, resulting in a parse tree showing their syntactic relation to each other, which may also contain semantic and other information.

The term is also used in psycholinguistics when describing language comprehension. In this context, parsing refers to the way that human beings analyze a sentence or phrase (in spoken language or text) "in terms of grammatical constituents, identifying the parts of speech, syntactic relations, etc." This term is especially common when discussing what linguistic cues help speakers to interpret garden-path sentences.

Within computer science, the term is used in the analysis of computer languages, referring to the syntactic analysis of the input code into its component parts in order to facilitate the writing of compilers and interpreters. The term may also be used to describe a split or separation.

Human Languages

Traditional Methods

The traditional grammatical exercise of parsing, sometimes known as *clause analysis*, involves breaking down a text into its component parts of speech with an explanation of the form, function, and syntactic relationship of each part. This is determined in large part from study of the language's conjugations and declensions, which can be quite intricate for heavily inflected languages. To parse a phrase such as 'man bites dog' involves noting that the singular noun 'man' is the subject of the sentence, the verb 'bites' is the third person singular of the present tense of the verb 'to bite', and the singular noun 'dog' is the object of the sentence. Techniques such as sentence diagrams are sometimes used to indicate relation between elements in the sentence.

Parsing was formerly central to the teaching of grammar throughout the English-speaking world, and widely regarded as basic to the use and understanding of written language. However, the general teaching of such techniques is no longer current.

Computational Methods

Normally parsing defined as separation. To separate the sentence into grammatical meaning or words, phrase, numbers. In some machine translation and natural language processing systems, written texts in human languages are parsed by computer programs. Human sentences are not easily parsed by programs, as there is substantial ambiguity in the structure of human language, whose usage is to convey meaning (or semantics) amongst a potentially unlimited range of possibilities but only some of which are germane to the particular case. So an utterance "Man bites dog" versus "Dog bites man" is definite on one detail but in another language might appear as "Man dog bites" with a reliance on the larger context to distinguish between those two possibilities, if indeed that difference was of concern. It is difficult to prepare formal rules to describe informal behaviour even though it is clear that some rules are being followed.

In order to parse natural language data, researchers must first agree on the grammar to be used. The choice of syntax is affected by both linguistic and computational concerns; for instance some parsing systems use lexical functional grammar, but in general, parsing for grammars of this type is known to be NP-complete. Head-driven phrase structure grammar is another linguistic formalism which has been popular in the parsing community, but other research efforts have focused on less complex formalisms such as the one used in the Penn Treebank. Shallow parsing aims to find only the boundaries of major constituents such as noun phrases. Another popular strategy for avoiding linguistic controversy is dependency grammar parsing.

Most modern parsers are at least partly statistical; that is, they rely on a corpus of training data which has already been annotated (parsed by hand). This approach allows the system to gather information about the frequency with which various constructions occur in specific contexts. Approaches which have been used include straightforward PCFGs (probabilistic context-free grammars), maximum entropy, and neural nets. Most of the more successful systems use *lexical* statistics (that is, they consider the identities of the words involved, as well as their part of speech). However such systems are vulnerable to overfitting and require some kind of smoothing to be effective.

Parsing algorithms for natural language cannot rely on the grammar having 'nice' properties as with manually designed grammars for programming languages. As mentioned earlier some grammar formalisms are very difficult to parse computationally; in general, even if the desired structure is not context-free, some kind of context-free approximation to the grammar is used to perform a first pass. Algorithms which use context-free grammars often rely on some variant of the CYK algorithm, usually with some heuristic to prune away unlikely analyses to save time. However some systems trade speed for accuracy using, e.g., linear-time versions of the shift-reduce algorithm. A somewhat recent development has been parse reranking in which the parser proposes some large number of analyses, and a more complex system selects the best option.

Psycholinguistics

In psycholinguistics, parsing involves not just the assignment of words to categories, but the evaluation of the meaning of a sentence according to the rules of syntax drawn by inferences made from each word in the sentence. This normally occurs as words are being heard or read. Consequently, psycholinguistic models of parsing are of necessity *incremental*, meaning that they build up an interpretation as the sentence is being processed, which is normally expressed in terms of a partial syntactic structure. Creation of initially wrong structures occurs when interpreting garden path sentences.

Computer Languages

Parser

A parser is a software component that takes input data (frequently text) and builds a data structure – often some kind of parse tree, abstract syntax tree or other hierarchical structure – giving a structural representation of the input, checking for correct syntax in the process. The parsing may be preceded or followed by other steps, or these may be combined into a single step. The parser is often preceded by a separate lexical analyser, which creates tokens from the sequence of input characters; alternatively, these can be combined in scannerless parsing. Parsers may be programmed by hand or may be automatically or semi-automatically generated by a parser generator. Parsing is complementary to templating, which produces formatted *output*. These may be applied to different domains, but often appear together, such as the scanf/printf pair, or the input (front end parsing) and output (back end code generation) stages of a compiler.

The input to a parser is often text in some computer language, but may also be text in a natural language or less structured textual data, in which case generally only certain parts of the text are extracted, rather than a parse tree being constructed. Parsers range from very simple functions such as scanf, to complex programs such as the frontend of a C++ compiler or the HTML parser of a web browser. An important class of simple parsing is done using regular expressions, in which a group of regular expressions defines a regular language and a regular expression engine automatically generating a parser for that language, allowing pattern matching and extraction of text. In other contexts regular expressions are instead used prior to parsing, as the lexing step whose output is then used by the parser.

The use of parsers varies by input. In the case of data languages, a parser is often found as the file reading facility of a program, such as reading in HTML or XML text; these examples are markup languages. In the case of programming languages, a parser is a component of a compiler or interpreter, which parses the source code of a computer programming language to create some form of internal representation; the parser is a key step in the compiler frontend. Programming languages tend to be specified in terms of a deterministic context-free grammar because fast and efficient parsers can be written for them. For compilers, the parsing itself can be done in one pass or multiple passes – see one-pass compiler and multi-pass compiler.

The implied disadvantages of a one-pass compiler can largely be overcome by adding fix-ups, where provision is made for fix-ups during the forward pass, and the fix-ups are applied backwards when the current program segment has been recognized as having been completed. An example where such a fix-up mechanism would be useful would be a forward GOTO statement, where the target of the GOTO is unknown until the program segment is completed. In this case, the application of the fix-up would be delayed until the target of the GOTO was recognized. Obviously, a backward GOTO does not require a fix-up.

Context-free grammars are limited in the extent to which they can express all of the requirements of a language. Informally, the reason is that the memory of such a language is limited. The grammar cannot remember the presence of a construct over an arbitrarily long input; this is necessary for a language in which, for example, a name must be declared before it may be referenced. More powerful grammars that can express this constraint, however, cannot be parsed efficiently. Thus, it is a common strategy to create a relaxed parser for a context-free grammar which accepts a superset of the desired language constructs (that is, it accepts some invalid constructs); later, the unwanted constructs can be filtered out at the semantic analysis (contextual analysis) step.

For example, in Python the following is syntactically valid code:

```
x = 1
print(x)
```

The following code, however, is syntactically valid in terms of the context-free grammar, yielding a syntax tree with the same structure as the previous, but is syntactically invalid in terms of the context-sensitive grammar, which requires that variables be initialized before use:

```
x = 1
print(y)
```

Rather than being analyzed at the parsing stage, this is caught by checking the *values* in the syntax tree, hence as part of *semantic* analysis: context-sensitive syntax is in practice often more easily analyzed as semantics.

Overview of Process

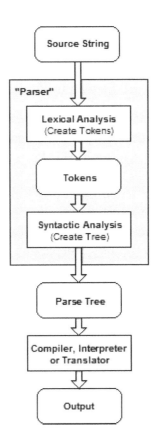

The following example demonstrates the common case of parsing a computer language with two levels of grammar: lexical and syntactic.

The first stage is the token generation, or lexical analysis, by which the input character stream is split into meaningful symbols defined by a grammar of regular expressions. For example, a calculator program would look at an input such as "12* (3+4) ^2" and split it into the tokens 12, *, (, 3, +, 4,), ^, 2, each of which is a meaningful symbol in the context of an arithmetic expression. The lexer would contain rules to tell it that the characters *, +, ^, (and) mark the start of a new token, so meaningless tokens like "12*" or "(3" will not be generated.

The next stage is parsing or syntactic analysis, which is checking that the tokens form an allowable expression. This is usually done with reference to a context-free grammar which recursively defines components that can make up an expression and the order in which they must appear. However, not all rules defining programming languages can be expressed by context-free grammars alone, for example type validity and proper declaration of identifiers. These rules can be formally expressed with attribute grammars.

The final phase is semantic parsing or analysis, which is working out the implications of the expression just validated and taking the appropriate action. In the case of a calculator or interpreter, the action is to evaluate the expression or program, a compiler, on the other hand, would generate some kind of code. Attribute grammars can also be used to define these actions.

Types of Parsers

The *task* of the parser is essentially to determine if and how the input can be derived from the start symbol of the grammar. This can be done in essentially two ways:

- Top-down parsing - Top-down parsing can be viewed as an attempt to find left-most derivations of an input-stream by searching for parse trees using a top-down expansion of the given formal grammar rules. Tokens are consumed from left to right. Inclusive choice is used to accommodate ambiguity by expanding all alternative right-hand-sides of grammar rules.

- Bottom-up parsing - A parser can start with the input and attempt to rewrite it to the start symbol. Intuitively, the parser attempts to locate the most basic elements, then the elements containing these, and so on. LR parsers are examples of bottom-up parsers. Another term used for this type of parser is Shift-Reduce parsing.

LL parsers and recursive-descent parser are examples of top-down parsers which cannot accommodate left recursive production rules. Although it has been believed that simple implementations of top-down parsing cannot accommodate direct and indirect left-recursion and may require exponential time and space complexity while parsing ambiguous context-free grammars, more sophisticated algorithms for top-down parsing have been created by Frost, Hafiz, and Callaghan which accommodate ambiguity and left recursion in polynomial time and which generate polynomial-size representations of the potentially exponential number of parse trees. Their algorithm is able to produce both left-most and right-most derivations of an input with regard to a given context-free grammar.

An important distinction with regard to parsers is whether a parser generates a *leftmost deriva-tion* or a *rightmost derivation*. LL parsers will generate a leftmost derivation and LR parsers will generate a rightmost derivation (although usually in reverse).

Parser Development Software

Some of the well known parser development tools include the following. Also see comparison of parser generators.

• ANTLR	• Parboiled
• Bison	• Parsec
• Coco/R	• Ragel
• GOLD	• Spirit Parser Framework
• JavaCC	• Syntax Definition Formalism
• Lemon	• SYNTAX
• Lex	• XPL
• LuZc	• Yacc

Lookahead

Lookahead establishes the maximum incoming tokens that a parser can use to decide which rule it should use. Lookahead is especially relevant to LL, LR, and LALR parsers, where it is often ex-plicitly indicated by affixing the lookahead to the algorithm name in parentheses, such as LALR(1).

Most programming languages, the primary target of parsers, are carefully defined in such a way that a parser with limited lookahead, typically one, can parse them, because parsers with limited lookahead are often more efficient. One important change to this trend came in 1990 when Ter-ence Parr created ANTLR for his Ph.D. thesis, a parser generator for efficient LL(k) parsers, where k is any fixed value.

Parsers typically have only a few actions after seeing each token. They are shift (add this token to the stack for later reduction), reduce (pop tokens from the stack and form a syntactic construct), end, error (no known rule applies) or conflict (does not know whether to shift or reduce).

Lookahead has two advantages.

- It helps the parser take the correct action in case of conflicts. For example, parsing the if statement in the case of an else clause.

- It eliminates many duplicate states and eases the burden of an extra stack. A C language non-lookahead parser will have around 10,000 states. A lookahead parser will have around 300 states.

Example: Parsing the Expression 1 + 2 * 3

Set of expression parsing rules (called grammar) is as follows,		
Rule1:	E → E + E	Expression is the sum of two expressions.
Rule2:	E → E * E	Expression is the product of two expressions.
Rule3:	E → number	Expression is a simple number
Rule4:	+ has less precedence than *	

Most programming languages (except for a few such as APL and Smalltalk) and algebraic formulas give higher precedence to multiplication than addition, in which case the correct interpretation of the example above is (1 + (2*3)). Note that Rule4 above is a semantic rule. It is possible to rewrite the grammar to incorporate this into the syntax. However, not all such rules can be translated into syntax.

Simple non-lookahead parser actions

Initially Input = [1,+,2,*,3]

1. Shift "1" onto stack from input (in anticipation of rule3). Input = [+,2,*,3] Stack =

2. Reduces "1" to expression "E" based on rule3. Stack = [E]

3. Shift "+" onto stack from input (in anticipation of rule1). Input = [2,*,3] Stack = [E,+]

4. Shift "2" onto stack from input (in anticipation of rule3). Input = [*,3] Stack = [E,+,2]

5. Reduce stack element "2" to Expression "E" based on rule3. Stack = [E,+,E]

6. Reduce stack items [E,+] and new input "E" to "E" based on rule1. Stack = [E]

7. Shift "*" onto stack from input (in anticipation of rule2). Input = Stack = [E,*]

8. Shift "3" onto stack from input (in anticipation of rule3). Input = [] (empty) Stack = [E,*,3]

9. Reduce stack element "3" to expression "E" based on rule3. Stack = [E,*,E]

10. Reduce stack items [E,*] and new input "E" to "E" based on rule2. Stack = [E]

The parse tree and resulting code from it is not correct according to language semantics.

To correctly parse without lookahead, there are three solutions:

- The user has to enclose expressions within parentheses. This often is not a viable solution.

- The parser needs to have more logic to backtrack and retry whenever a rule is violated or not complete. The similar method is followed in LL parsers.

- Alternatively, the parser or grammar needs to have extra logic to delay reduction and reduce only when it is absolutely sure which rule to reduce first. This method is used in LR parsers. This correctly parses the expression but with many more states and increased stack depth.

Lookahead parser actions

1. Shift 1 onto stack on input 1 in anticipation of rule3. It does not reduce immediately.

2. Reduce stack item 1 to simple Expression on input + based on rule3. The lookahead is +, so we are on path to E +, so we can reduce the stack to E.

3. Shift + onto stack on input + in anticipation of rule1.

4. Shift 2 onto stack on input 2 in anticipation of rule3.

5. Reduce stack item 2 to Expression on input * based on rule3. The lookahead * expects only E before it.

6. Now stack has E + E and still the input is *. It has two choices now, either to shift based on rule2 or reduction based on rule1. Since * has higher precedence than + based on rule4, we shift * onto stack in anticipation of rule2.

7. Shift 3 onto stack on input 3 in anticipation of rule3.

8. Reduce stack item 3 to Expression after seeing end of input based on rule3.

9. Reduce stack items E * E to E based on rule2.

10. Reduce stack items E + E to E based on rule1.

The parse tree generated is correct and simply more efficient than non-lookahead parsers. This is the strategy followed in LALR parsers.

Top Down Parsing

*   Following grammar generates types of Pascal

type ⟶ simple

  |↑id

  | array [simple] of type

simple ⟶ integer

  | char

  | num dotdot num

Top-down parsing is a strategy of analyzing unknown data relationships by hypothesizing general parse tree structures and then considering whether the known fundamental structures are compatible with the hypothesis. For example, the following grammar generates the types in Pascal language by starting from type and generating the string:

type ⟶ simple

  |↑id

  | array [simple] of type

simple ⟶ integer

| char

| num dotdot num

ANTLR

In computer-based language recognition, ANTLR (pronounced *Antler*), or Another Tool For Language Recognition, is a parser generator that uses LL(*) for parsing. ANTLR is the successor to the Purdue Compiler Construction Tool Set (PCCTS), first developed in 1989, and is under active development. Its maintainer is Professor Terence Parr of the University of San Francisco.

Usage

ANTLR takes as input a grammar that specifies a language and generates as output source code for a recognizer for that language. While version 3 supported generating code in the programming languages Ada95, ActionScript, C, C#, Java, JavaScript, Objective-C, Perl, Python, Ruby, and Standard ML, the current release at present only targets Java, C#, JavaScript, Python2, Python3, Swift, Go. A new, C++ target also exists. A language is specified using a context-free grammar which is expressed using Extended Backus–Naur Form (EBNF).

ANTLR can generate lexers, parsers, tree parsers, and combined lexer-parsers. Parsers can automatically generate parse trees or abstract syntax trees which can be further processed with tree parsers. ANTLR provides a single consistent notation for specifying lexers, parsers, and tree parsers. This is in contrast with other parser/lexer generators and adds greatly to the tool's ease of use.

By default, ANTLR reads a grammar and generates a recognizer for the language defined by the grammar (i.e. a program that reads an input stream and generates an error if the input stream does not conform to the syntax specified by the grammar). If there are no syntax errors, then the default action is to simply exit without printing any message. In order to do something useful with the language, actions can be attached to grammar elements in the grammar. These actions are written in the programming language in which the recognizer is being generated. When the recognizer is being generated, the actions are embedded in the source code of the recognizer at the appropriate points. Actions can be used to build and check symbol tables and to emit instructions in a target language, in the case of a compiler.

As well as lexers and parsers, ANTLR can be used to generate tree parsers. These are recognizers that process abstract syntax trees which can be automatically generated by parsers. These tree parsers are unique to ANTLR and greatly simplify the processing of abstract syntax trees.

Licensing

ANTLR 3 is free software, published under a three-clause BSD License. Prior versions were released as public domain software. The book *The Definitive ANTLR 4 Reference*, also written by Parr, is available free for charge in source form.

Various plugins have been developed for the Eclipse development environment to support the

ANTLR grammar, including ANTLR Studio, a proprietary product, as well as the "ANTLR 2" and "ANTLR 3" plugins for Eclipse hosted on Source Forge.

ANTLR 4

ANTLR 4 deals with left recursion correctly (except for indirect left recursion, i.e. grammars rules x which refer to y which refer to x) and supports actions and attributes flexibly. That is, actions can be defined separately from the grammar, allowing for easier targeting of multiple languages.

Projects

Here is a non-comprehensive list of software built using ANTLR:

- Groovy
- Jython
- Hibernate
- OpenJDK Compiler Grammar project experimental version of the javac compiler based upon a grammar written in ANTLR
- Apex, Salesforce.com's programming language
- The expression evaluator in Numbers, Apple's spreadsheet
- Twitter's search query language
- Weblogic server
- IntelliJ IDEA and Clion.
- Apache Cassandra
- Processing
- JabRef

Example

In the following example, a parser in ANTLR describes the sum of expressions can be seen in the form of "1 + 2 + 3":

```
// Common options, for example, the target language
 options
 {
  language = "CSharp";
 }
// Followed by the parser
 class SumParser extends Parser;
```

```
options
{
  k = 1; // Parser Lookahead: 1 Token
}
// Definition of an expression
statement: INTEGER (PLUS^ INTEGER)*;
// Here is the Lexer
class SumLexer extends Lexer;
options
{
  k = 1; // Lexer Lookahead: 1 characters
}
PLUS: '+';
DIGIT: ('0'..'9');
INTEGER: (DIGIT)+;
```

The following listing demonstrates the call of the parser in a program:

```
TextReader reader;
// (...) Fill TextReader with character
SumLexer lexer = new SumLexer(reader);
SumParser parser = new SumParser(lexer);
parser.expression();
```

Flex (Lexical Analyser Generator)

Flex (fast lexical analyzer generator) is a free and open-source software alternative to lex. It is a computer program that generates lexical analyzers (also known as "scanners" or "lexers"). It is frequently used as the lex implementation together with Berkeley Yacc parser generator on BSD-derived operating systems (as both lex and yacc are part of POSIX), or together with GNU bison (a version of yacc) in *BSD ports and in Linux distributions. Unlike Bison, flex is not part of the GNU Project and is not released under the GNU General Public License.

History

Flex was written in C by Vern Paxson around 1987. He was translating a Ratfor generator, which had been led by Jef Poskanzer.

Example lexical analyzer

This is an example of a Flex scanner for the instructional programming language PL/0.

The tokens recognized are: '+', '-', '*', '/', '=', '(', ')', ',', ';', '.', ':=', '<', '<=', '<>', '>', '>='; numbers: 0-9 {0-9}; identifiers: a-zA-Z {a-zA-Z0-9} and keywords: begin, call, const, do, end, if, odd, procedure, then, var, while.

```
%{

#include "y.tab.h"

%}


digit          [0-9]
letter         [a-zA-Z]


%%
"+"                    { return PLUS;        }

"-"                    { return MINUS;       }

"*"                    { return TIMES;       }

"/"                    { return SLASH;       }

"("                    { return LPAREN;      }

")"                    { return RPAREN;      }

";"                    { return SEMICOLON;   }

","                    { return COMMA;       }

"."                    { return PERIOD;      }

":="                   { return BECOMES;     }

"="                    { return EQL;         }

"<>"                   { return NEQ;         }

"<"                    { return LSS;         }

">"                    { return GTR;         }

"<="                   { return LEQ;         }

">="                   { return GEQ;         }

"begin"                { return BEGINSYM;    }

"call"                 { return CALLSYM;     }

"const"                { return CONSTSYM;    }

"do"                   { return DOSYM;       }

"end"                  { return ENDSYM;      }

"if"                   { return IFSYM;       }

"odd"                  { return ODDSYM;      }
```

```
"procedure"            { return PROCSYM;     }

"then"                 { return THENSYM;     }

"var"                  { return VARSYM;      }

"while"                { return WHILESYM;    }

{letter}({letter}|{digit})* {

                       yylval.id = strdup(yytext);

                       return IDENT;         }

{digit}+               { yylval.num = atoi(yytext);

                       return NUMBER;        }

[ \t\n\r]              /* skip whitespace */

.                      { printf("Unknown character [%c]\n",yytext);

                       return UNKNOWN;       }

%%

int yywrap(void){return 1;}
```

Internals

These programs perform character parsing and tokenizing via the use of a deterministic finite automaton (DFA). A DFA is a theoretical machine accepting regular languages. These machines are a subset of the collection of Turing machines. DFAs are equivalent to read-only right moving Turing machines. The syntax is based on the use of regular expressions.

Issues

Time Complexity

A Flex lexical analyzer usually has time complexity $O(n)$ in the length of the input. That is, it performs a constant number of operations for each input symbol. This constant is quite low: GCC generates 12 instructions for the DFA match loop. Note that the constant is independent of the length of the token, the length of the regular expression and the size of the DFA.

However, using the REJECT macro in a scanner with the potential to match extremely long tokens can cause Flex to generate a scanner with non-linear performance. This feature is optional. In this case, the programmer has explicitly told Flex to "go back and try again" after it has already matched some input. This will cause the DFA to backtrack to find other accept states. The REJECT feature is not enabled by default, and because of its performance implications its use is discouraged in the Flex manual.

Reentrancy

By default the scanner generated by Flex is not reentrant. This can cause serious problems for programs that use the generated scanner from different threads. To overcome this issue there are options that Flex provides in order to achieve reentrancy. A detailed description of these options can be found in the Flex manual.

Usage Under Non-unix Environments

Normally the generated scanner contains references to *unistd.h* header file which is Unix specific. To avoid generating code that includes *unistd.h*, *%option nounistd* should be used. Another issue is the call to *isatty* (a Unix library function), which can be found in the generated code. The *%option never-interactive* forces flex to generate code that doesn't use *isatty*.

Using Flex From Other Languages

Flex can only generate code for C and C++. To use the scanner code generated by flex from other languages a language binding tool such as SWIG can be used.

Flex++

flex++ is a similar lexical scanner for C++ which is included as part of the flex package. The generated code does not depend on any runtime or external library except for a memory allocator (malloc or a user-supplied alternative) unless the input also depends on it. This can be useful in embedded and similar situations where traditional operating system or C runtime facilities may not be available.

The flex++ generated C++ scanner includes the header file FlexLexer.h, which defines the interfaces of the two C++ generated classes.

References

- "Code-Level And API Options - Lexical Analysis With Flex, for Flex 2.5.37". Flex.sourceforge.net. Retrieved 2013-02-25

- James Gosling (2000). The Java Language Specification. Addison-Wesley Professional. pp. 9–. ISBN 978-0-201-31008-5

- Perl 5 Porters. "perlinterp: Perl 5 version 24.0 documentation". perldoc.perl.org - Official documentation for the Perl programming language. perldoc.perl.org. Retrieved 26 January 2017

- Guy Coder (19 February 2013). "What is the difference between token and lexeme?". Stack Overflow. Stack Exchange Inc. Retrieved 26 January 2017

- Buyya (2009). Object-oriented Programming with Java: Essentials and Applications. Tata McGraw-Hill Education. pp. 57–. ISBN 978-0-07-066908-6

- Kochurkin, Ivan (27 July 2016). "Tree structures processing and unified AST". Positive Research Center. Retrieved 5 August 2016

- Bumbulis, P.; Cowan, D. D. (Mar–Dec 1993). "RE2C: A more versatile scanner generator". ACM Letters on Programming Languages and Systems. 2 (1–4): 70–84. doi:10.1145/176454.176487

An Integrated Study of Intermediate Representation

The code used by a compiler to represent a source code is referred to as intermediate representation. A good intermediate representation needs to be accurate so that it can represent the source code without losing any information. Intermediate representation is an interdisciplinary subject. It spreads to other fields as well. This chapter will provide a glimpse of related fields of intermediate representation briefly.

Intermediate Representation

An Intermediate representation (IR) is the data structure or code used internally by a compiler or virtual machine to represent source code. An IR is designed to be conducive for further processing, such as optimization and translation. A "good" IR must be *accurate* – capable of representing the source code without loss of information – and *independent* of any particular source or target language. An IR may take one of several forms: an in-memory data structure, or a special tuple- or stack-based code readable by the program. In the latter case it is also called an *intermediate language*.

A canonical example is found in most modern compilers, where the linear human-readable text representing a program is transformed into an intermediate graph structure that allows flow analysis and re-arrangement before creating a sequence of actual CPU instructions. Use of an intermediate representation such as this allows compiler systems like the GNU Compiler Collection and LLVM to be used by many different source languages to generate code for many different target architectures.

Intermediate Language

An intermediate language is the language of an abstract machine designed to aid in the analysis of computer programs. The term comes from their use in compilers, where the source code of a program is translated into a form more suitable for code-improving transformations before being used to generate object or machine code for a target machine. The design of an intermediate language typically differs from that of a practical machine language in three fundamental ways:

- Each instruction represents exactly one fundamental operation; *e.g.* "shift-add" addressing modes common in microprocessors are not present.

- Control flow information may not be included in the instruction set.

- The number of processor registers available may be large, even limitless.

A popular format for intermediate languages is three-address code.

The term is also used to refer to languages used as intermediates by some high-level programming languages which do not output object or machine code themselves, but output the intermediate language only. This intermediate language is submitted to a compiler for such language, which then outputs finished object or machine code. This is usually done to ease the process of optimization or to increase portability by using an intermediate language that has compilers for many processors and operating systems, such as C. Languages used for this fall in complexity between high-level languages and low-level languages, such as assembly languages.

Languages

Though not explicitly designed as an intermediate language, C's nature as an abstraction of assembly and its ubiquity as the de facto system language in Unix-like and other operating systems has made it a popular intermediate language: Eiffel, Sather, Esterel, some dialects of Lisp (Lush, Gambit), Haskell (Glasgow Haskell Compiler), Squeak's Smalltalk-subset Slang, Cython, Seed7, SystemTap, Vala, and others make use of C as an intermediate language. Variants of C have been designed to provide C's features as a portable assembly language, including C-- and the C Intermediate Language.

Any language targeting a virtual machine or p-code machine can be considered an intermediate language:

- Java bytecode

- Microsoft's Common Intermediate Language is an intermediate language designed to be shared by all compilers for the .NET Framework, before static or dynamic compilation to machine code.

- While most intermediate languages are designed to support statically typed languages, the Parrot intermediate representation is designed to support dynamically typed languages—initially Perl and Python.

- TIMI is a high level that targets the IBM System i platform.

- O-code for BCPL

- MATLAB precompiled code

- Microsoft P-Code

The GNU Compiler Collection (GCC) uses several intermediate languages internally to simplify portability and cross-compilation. Among these languages are

- the historical Register Transfer Language (RTL)

- the tree language GENERIC

- the SSA-based GIMPLE.

- Standard Portable Intermediate Representation SPIR/SPIR-V

- LLVM Intermediate Representation

- HSA Intermediate Layer

The LLVM compiler framework is based on the LLVM IR intermediate language, which has been productized by Apple as "bitcode".

The ILOC intermediate language is used in classes on compiler design as a simple target language.

Other

Static analysis tools often use an intermediate representation. For instance, radare2 is a toolbox for binary files analysis and reverse-engineering. It uses the intermediate languages ESIL et REIL to analyze binary files.

Static Program Analysis

Static program analysis is the analysis of computer software that is performed without actually executing programs (analysis performed on executing programs is known as dynamic analysis). In most cases the analysis is performed on some version of the source code, and in the other cases, some form of the object code.

The term is usually applied to the analysis performed by an automated tool, with human analysis being called program understanding, program comprehension, or code review. Software inspections and software walkthroughs are also used in the latter case.

Rationale

The sophistication of the analysis performed by tools varies from those that only consider the behaviour of individual statements and declarations, to those that include the complete source code of a program in their analysis. The uses of the information obtained from the analysis vary from highlighting possible coding errors (e.g., the lint tool) to formal methods that mathematically prove properties about a given program (e.g., its behaviour matches that of its specification).

Software metrics and reverse engineering can be described as forms of static analysis. Deriving software metrics and static analysis are increasingly deployed together, especially in creation of embedded systems, by defining so-called *software quality objectives*.

A growing commercial use of static analysis is in the verification of properties of software used in safety-critical computer systems and locating potentially vulnerable code. For example, the following industries have identified the use of static code analysis as a means of improving the quality of increasingly sophisticated and complex software:

1. Medical software: The U.S. Food and Drug Administration (FDA) has identified the use of static analysis for medical devices.

2. Nuclear software: In the UK the Office for Nuclear Regulation (ONR) recommends the use of static analysis on reactor protection systems.

3. Aviation software (in combination with dynamic analysis)

A study in 2012 by VDC Research reports that 28.7% of the embedded software engineers surveyed currently use static analysis tools and 39.7% expect to use them within 2 years. A study from 2010 found that 60% of the interviewed developers in European research projects made at least use of their basic IDE built-in static analyzers. However, only about 10% employed an additional other (and perhaps more advanced) analysis tool.

In the application security industry the name *Static Application Security Testing* (SAST) is also used. Actually, SAST is an important part of Security Development Lifecycles (SDLs) such as the SDL defined by Microsoft and a common practice in software companies.

Tool Types

The OMG (Object Management Group) published a study regarding the types of software analysis required for software quality measurement and assessment. This document on "How to Deliver Resilient, Secure, Efficient, and Easily Changed IT Systems in Line with CISQ Recommendations" describes three levels of software analysis.

Unit Level

> Analysis that takes place within a specific program or subroutine, without connecting to the context of that program.

Technology Level

> Analysis that takes into account interactions between unit programs to get a more holistic and semantic view of the overall program in order to find issues and avoid obvious false positives.

System Level

> Analysis that takes into account the interactions between unit programs, but without being limited to one specific technology or programming language.

A further level of software analysis can be defined.

Mission/Business Level

> Analysis that takes into account the business/mission layer terms, rules and processes that are implemented within the software system for its operation as part of enterprise or program/mission layer activities. These elements are implemented without being limited to one specific technology or programming language and in many cases are distributed across multiple languages, but are statically extracted and analyzed for system understanding for mission assurance.

Formal Methods

Formal methods is the term applied to the analysis of software (and computer hardware) whose results are obtained purely through the use of rigorous mathematical methods. The mathematical techniques used include denotational semantics, axiomatic semantics, operational semantics, and abstract interpretation.

By a straightforward reduction to the halting problem, it is possible to prove that (for any Turing complete language), finding all possible run-time errors in an arbitrary program (or more generally any kind of violation of a specification on the final result of a program) is undecidable: there is no mechanical method that can always answer truthfully whether an arbitrary program may or may not exhibit runtime errors. This result dates from the works of Church, Gödel and Turing in the 1930s. As with many undecidable questions, one can still attempt to give useful approximate solutions.

Some of the implementation techniques of formal static analysis include:

- Abstract interpretation, to model the effect that every statement has on the state of an abstract machine (i.e., it 'executes' the software based on the mathematical properties of each statement and declaration). This abstract machine over-approximates the behaviours of the system: the abstract system is thus made simpler to analyze, at the expense of *incompleteness* (not every property true of the original system is true of the abstract system). If properly done, though, abstract interpretation is *sound* (every property true of the abstract system can be mapped to a true property of the original system). The Frama-C value analysis plugin and Polyspace heavily rely on abstract interpretation.

- Data-flow analysis, a lattice-based technique for gathering information about the possible set of values;

- Hoare logic, a formal system with a set of logical rules for reasoning rigorously about the correctness of computer programs. There is tool support for some programming languages (e.g., the SPARK programming language (a subset of Ada) and the Java Modeling Language — JML — using ESC/Java and ESC/Java2, Frama-C WP (weakest precondition) plugin for the C language extended with ACSL (ANSI/ISO C Specification Language)).

- Model checking, considers systems that have finite state or may be reduced to finite state by abstraction;

- Symbolic execution, as used to derive mathematical expressions representing the value of mutated variables at particular points in the code.

Intermediate Representation Design

- More of a wizardry rather than science
- each compiler uses 2-3 IRs
- HIR (high level IR) preserves loop structure and array bounds
- MIR (medium level IR) reflects range of features in a set of source languages
  - language independent
  - good for code generation for one or more architectures
  - appropriate for most optimizations

- LIR (low level IR) low level similar to the machines

Intermediate Representation (IR) is language-independent and machine-independent. A good intermediate representation can be said as one which:

- Captures high level language constructs,

- Should be easy to translate from abstract syntax tree,

- Should support high-level optimizations,

- Captures low-level machine features,

- Should be easy to translate to assembly,

- Should support machine-dependent optimizations,

- Has narrower interface i.e. small number of node types (instructions), and

- Should be easy to optimize and retarget .

To design such an IR having all these features is a very difficult task. Thus most compliers use multiple IRs. So, various optimizations are done by different IRs and are easy to implement and extend.

For this, IR can be categorized into 3 types:

1. High Level IR (HIR): This is language independent but closer to the high level language. HIR preserves high-level language constructs such as structured control flows: if, for, while, etc; variables, expressions, functions etc. It also allows high level optimizations depending on the source language, e.g., function inlining, memory dependence analysis, loop transformations, etc.

for v <- v1 by v2 to v3 do

a[v]:=2

endfor

2. Medium Level IR (MIR): This is machine and language independent and can represent a set of source languages. Thus MIR is good for code generation for one or more architectures. It utilizes simple control flow structure like "if" and "goto"; allows source language variables (human form names) as well as front-end created "temporaries" (symbolic registers). Compared to HIR, it reveals computations in greater detail (much closer to the machine than HIR), and therefore is usually preferred for needs of optimization.

The HIR Example is translated into the following MIR code:

    v <- v1

    t2 <- v2

    t3 <- v3

L1:

    if v > t3 goto L2

    t4 <- addr a

    t5 <- 4 * v

    t6 <- t4 + t5

    *t6 <- 2

    v <- v + t2

    goto L1

    L2:

3. Low Level IR (LIR): This is machine independent but more closer to the machine (e.g., RTL used in GCC). It is easy to generate code from LIR but generation of input program may involve some work. LIR has low level constructs such as unstructured jumps, registers, memory locations. LIR has features of MIR and LIR. It can also have features of HIR depending on the needs. The LIR code for the above MIR example is:

    s2 <- s1

    s4 <- s3

    s6 <- s5

L1:

    if s2 > s6 goto L2

    s7 <- addr a

    s8 <- 4 * s9

    s10 <- s7 + s8

    [s10] <- 2

    s2 <- s2 + s4

    goto L1

L2:

- Compiler writers have tried to define Universal IRs and have failed. (UNCOL in 1958)

- There is no standard Intermediate Representation. IR is a step in expressing a source program so that machine understands it

- As the translation takes place, IR is repeatedly analyzed and transformed

- Compiler users want analysis and translation to be fast and correct

- Compiler writers want optimizations to be simple to write, easy to understand and easy to extend

- IR should be simple and light weight while allowing easy expression of optimizations and transformations.

Compiler writers have tried to define Universal IRs and have failed . UNCOL , UNiversal Computer Oriented Language, was a proposed universal language for compilers . It was discussed but never implemented. UNCOL would have supported a back-end for every machine architecture. A compiler for a new programming language would only have to compile to UNCOL. Everybody knows that UNCOL was a failure. As of now, there is no standard Intermediate Representation. A significant part of the compiler is both language and machine independent.

There are many issues in choosing an IR:

- Analysis and translation should be fast and correct.

- Writing an IR should be simple for compiler writers.

- IR should be easy to understand and easy to extend.

- It should be light weight and should allow optimizations and translation easily.

Issues in IR Design

- source language and target language

- porting cost or reuse of existing design

- whether appropriate for optimizations

- U-code IR used on PA-RISC and Mips. Suitable for expression evaluation on stacks but less suited for load- store architectures

- both compilers translate U-code to another form

  - HP translates to very low level representation

  - Mips translates to MIR and translates back to U-code for code generator

IR design is very much dependent on both the source language and the target language. There are many factors while choosing an intermediate language such as porting cost and reuse of existing design i.e., whether is it economical to reuse the existing design or rather redo from scratch. Here, portability mainly refers to machine-independence, rather than source-language independence. Also, will the IR be appropriate for the optimizations needed.

Complexity of the compiler: reuse of legacy compiler parts, compilation cost, multiple vs. one IR levels (as mentioned, a compiler may use several IRs from different levels, or a single IR featuring several levels), and compiler maintenance.

To emphasize the latter claim, here are two examples of implementation of optimization in the MIPS and the PA-RISC. Don't give too much attention to the examples as of now. Just try to get a hang of what's being said.

1. MIPS The problem introduced was how to optimize the front-end generated representation, namely UCODE Stack Based IR (a language that was something like an old instance of Java Byte-Code, which served as a target language for many front-ends). Given that the translation from UCODE to machine code ("load"/"store" based architecture) was already written, and since the required optimization used a higher-level representation, what was finally implemented is as follows: Ironically, this solution translates into a higher-level representation, performs the required optimizations, and then translates back to the low- level representation, from which the machine code is generated. Note, however, that we assume here that translation from one representation to another is accurate (but not necessarily efficient).

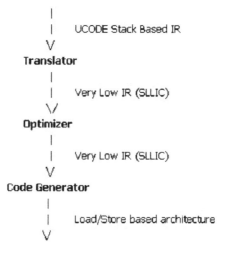

2. PA-RISC The second example shows a similar design for PA-RISC (developed by HP), but such that is using a lower-level IR (SLLIC) for optimization and doesn't translate back to UCODE.

3. This is schematically represented as follows:

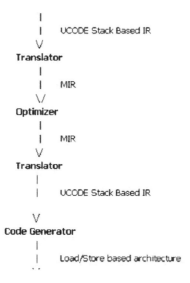

Issues in new IR Design

- how much machine dependent

- expressiveness: how many languages are covered

- appropriateness for code optimization

- appropriateness for code generation

- Use more than one IR (like in PA-RISC)

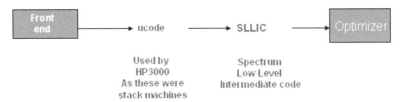

The issues in an IR design are:

1. Machine dependence: for machine level optimizations.

2. Expressiveness: for ease of understanding and extensibility.

3. Appropriateness for code optimization.

4. Appropriateness for code generation.

5. Whether it will use existing design or not? This is an important issue as if optimum; it should use pre-existing design so that it doesn't have issues of portability with previously existing architectures, and other issues.

6. Use of more than one IR for more optimization: Different IRs have different levels of optimizations possible.

7. Suitable for dependence analysis by representing subscripts by list of subscripts.

8. Make addresses explicit in linearized form. This is suitable for constant folding, strength reduction, loop invariant code motion and other basic optimizations.

- Use more than one IR for more than one optimization

- represent subscripts by list of subscripts: suitable for dependence analysis

- make addresses explicit in linearized form:

    - suitable for constant folding, strength reduction, loop invariant code motion, other basic optimizations

float a; use a[i][j+2]

HIR	MIR	LIR
t1 ⟵ a[i,j+2]	t1 ⟵ j+2	r1 ⟵ [fp-4]
	t2 ⟵ i*20	r2 ⟵ r1+2

	$t3 \leftarrow t1+t2$		$r3 \leftarrow [fp-8]$	
	$t4 \leftarrow 4*t3$		$r4 \leftarrow r3*20$	
	$t5 \leftarrow addr\ a$		$r5 \leftarrow r4+r2$	
	$t6 \leftarrow t4+t5$		$r6 \leftarrow 4*r5$	
	$t7 \leftarrow *t6$		$r7 \leftarrow fp-216$	
			$f1 \leftarrow [r7+r6]$	

This example shows the representation of the same code in three different IRs, all at different levels of abstraction. In the MIR, the size of the float and the array is used along with the address of the variable a . In the LIR, we are dealing with registers and file pointers instead (lower level of abstraction).

High level IR

int f(int a, int b) {

    int c;

    c = a + 2; print(b, c);

}

- Abstract syntax tree

    - keeps enough information to reconstruct source form

    - keeps information about symbol table

Consider the code given above. We will be showing the corresponding Abstract Syntax tree (AST) corresponding. An Abstract Syntax tree (a form of HIR) is used to generate the medium or low level intermediate language. We can also generate the original source form from the AST.

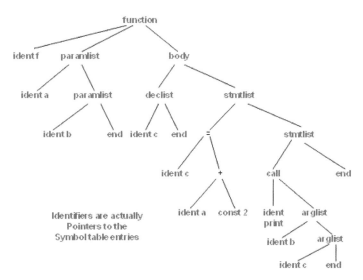

An abstract syntax tree (AST) is a finite , labeled, directed tree, where the nodes are labeled by operators, and the edges represent the operands of the node operators. Thus, the leaves have nullary operators, i.e., pointers to the symbol table entries of the variables or constants. An AST differs from a parse tree by omitting nodes and edges for syntax rules that do not affect the semantics of the program. The classic example of such an omission is grouping parentheses, since in an AST the grouping of operands is explicit in the tree structure.

- Medium level IR
    - reflects range of features in a set of source languages
    - language independent
    - good for code generation for a number of architectures
    - appropriate for most of the optimizations
    - normally three address code
- Low level IR
    - corresponds one to one to target machine instructions
    - architecture dependent
- Multi-level IR
    - has features of MIR and LIR
    - may also have some features of HIR

MIR

Many optimizations are based on this level of representation. It is characterized by the following:

- Source-language and target-machine independent: this is the commonly claimed advantage of MIR.
- Machine independent representation for program variables and temporaries.
- Simplified control flow construct.
- Portable (immediate outcome of source and target independence). Hence, good for code generation for a number of architectures. . Sufficient in many optimizing compilers: MIR, Sun-IR, etc.

LIR

Key characteristics:

- One-to-one correspondence with machine instructions (this is not 100% accurate, but is a major design issue).

- Deviations from machine language: alternative code for non-primitive operations (e.g., MULTIPLY); addressing modes; side effects (e.g., auto-increment by the machine that is not suitably represented).

- It is machine dependant. However, appropriate compiler data structures can hide machine dependence, for example: register allocation can be kept for the very last phase, thus we can still use symbolic register.

Multi-level IR

Key characteristics:

- Combining multiple representations levels in the same language: this way we hope to benefit from the advantages of some IRs for different optimization needs.

- Compromise computation exposure and high-level description (clearly, since we take some from high and low levels).

- Examples: in SUN-IR arrays can be represented with multiple subscripts; in SLLIC, MULTIPLY and DIVIDE operations exist.

Abstract Syntax Tree/DAG

- Condensed form of a parse tree

- useful for representing language constructs

- Depicts the natural hierarchical structure of the source program

    - Each internal node represents an operator

    - Children of the nodes represent operands

    - Leaf nodes represent operands

- DAG is more compact than abstract syntax tree because common sub expressions are eliminated

A syntax tree depicts the natural hierarchical structure of a source program.

DAGs are generated as a combination of trees: operands that are being reused are linked together, and nodes may be annotated with variable names (to denote assignments). This way, DAGs are highly compact, since they eliminate local common sub-expressions. On the other hand, they are not so easy to optimize, since they are more specific tree forms. However, it can be seen that proper building of DAG for a given sequence of instructions can compactly represent the outcome of the calculation.

An example of a syntax tree and DAG.

a := b * -c + b * -c

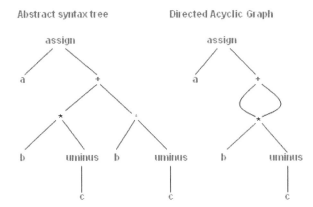

You can see that the node " * " comes only once in the DAG as well as the leaf " b ", but the meaning conveyed by both the representations (AST as well as the DAG) remains the same.

Postfix Notation

- Linearized representation of a syntax tree

- List of nodes of the tree

- Nodes appear immediately after its children

- The postfix notation for an expression E is defined as follows:

    - If E is a variable or constant then the postfix notation is E itself

    - If E is an expression of the form E 1 op E 2 where op is a binary operator then the postfix notation for E is

- E 1 ' E 2 ' op where E 1 ' and E 2 ' are the postfix notations for E 1 and E 2 respectively

    - If E is an expression of the form (E 1) then the postfix notation for E 1 is also the postfix notation for E

At some point in your career you will be asked to write a program that can interpret an expression in a notation similar to that of algebra. Getting something like (A+B)/(C- D) right can seem like a daunting task, especially when you are asked to write code that will interpret any valid expression. It turns out to be surprisingly easy if the program is decomposed into two steps: translation to postfix notation and evaluation of the postfix notation expression. This is not a new idea... it was described by Donald Knuth in 1962 and he was writing a history!

Postfix notation is a way of writing algebraic expressions without the use of parentheses or rules of operator precedence. The expression above would be written as AB+CD-/ in postfix notation. (Don't panic! We'll explain this in a moment.) Postfix notation had its beginnings in the work of Jan L ukasiewicz * (1878-1956), a Polish logician, mathematician, and philosopher. L ukasiewicz developed a parenthesis-free prefix notation that came to be called Polish notation and a postfix notation now called Reverse Polish Notation or RPN. From these ideas, Charles Hamblin developed a postfix notation for use in computers. L ukasiewicz's work dates from about 1920. Hamblin's work on postfix notation was in the mid-1950's. Calculators, notably those from Hewlett-Packard, used various postfix formats beginning in the 1960s.

Postfix notation is a linearized representation of a syntax tree; it is a list of nodes of the tree which appear immediately after its children. You must read the three points written in the slide above to see how postfix expressions are made corresponding to a set of expressions.

- No parenthesis are needed in postfix notation because

  - the position and parity of the operators permit only one decoding of a postfix expression

- Postfix notation for

  $a = b * -c + b * -c$

is

  $a b c - * b c - * + =$

No parenthesis is needed in postfix notation because it is made in a way that it has only one unique decoding. The parity of the operators (number of operands an operator takes) and their position uniquely determine the decoding.

Have a look at the postfix notation example given above. We had made the AST and DAG for this example a couple of slides back. The edges in a syntax tree do not appear explicitly in postfix notation. They can be recovered from the order in which the nodes (operators) appear and the number of operands that the operators at the nodes expect. The recovery of edges is similar to the evaluation, using a stack, of an expression in postfix notation.

Three Address Code

- It is a sequence of statements of the general form X := Y op Z where

  - X, Y or Z are names, constants or compiler generated temporaries

  - op stands for any operator such as a fixed- or floating-point arithmetic operator, or a logical operator

Three address code is a sequence of statements of the general form: x := y op z where x, y and z are names, constants, or compiler generated temporaries. op stands for any operator, such as a fixed or floating-point arithmetic operator, or a logical operator or boolean - valued data. Compilers use this form in their IR.

- Only one operator on the right hand side is allowed

- Source expression like x + y * z might be translated into

$t 1 := y * z$

$t 2 := x + t 1$

where t 1 and t 2 are compiler generated temporary names

- Unraveling of complicated arithmetic expressions and of control flow makes 3-address code desirable for code generation and optimization

- The use of names for intermediate values allows 3-address code to be easily rearranged

- Three address code is a linearized representation of a syntax tree where explicit names correspond to the interior nodes of the graph

Note that no built-up arithmetic expressions are permitted, as there is only one operator on the right side. Its advantage is that it can be easily rearranged. Each statement usually contains three addresses, two for the operands and one for the result. It is a linearized representation of a syntax tree in which explicit names correspond to the interior nodes of the graph. Variable names can appear directly in three address statements, so there are no statements corresponding to the leaves. The various types of the three-address code.

Three Address Instructions

. Assignment	. Function
- x = y op z	- param x
- x = op y	- call p,n
- x = y	- return y
. Jump	
- goto L	. Pointer
- if x relop y goto L	- x = &y
.Indexed assignment	- x = *y
- x = y[i]	- *x = y
- x[i] = y	

The various types of the three-address codes. Statements can have symbolic label and there are statements for flow of control. A symbolic label represents the index of a three-address statement in the array holding intermediate code. Actual indices can be substituted for the labels either by making a separate pass, or by using backpatching.

Other Representations

- SSA: Single Static Assignment

- RTL: Register transfer language

- Stack machines: P-code

- CFG: Control Flow Graph

- Dominator Trees

- DJ-graph: dominator tree augmented with join edges

- PDG: Program Dependence Graph

- VDG: Value Dependence Graph

- GURRR: Global unified resource requirement representation. Combines PDG with re-source requirements

- Java intermediate bytecodes

- The list goes on ......

These are some other types of representations that the compilers use.

Symbol Table

- Compiler uses symbol table to keep track of scope and binding information about names

- symbol table is changed every time a name is encountered in the source; changes to table occur

  - if a new name is discovered

  - if new information about an existing name is discovered

- Symbol table must have mechanism to:

  - add new entries

  - find existing information efficiently

- Two common mechanism:

  - linear lists, simple to implement, poor performance

  - hash tables, greater programming/space overhead, good performance

- Compiler should be able to grow symbol table dynamically

- if size is fixed, it must be large enough for the largest program

A compiler uses a symbol table to keep track of scope and binding information about names. It is filled after the AST is made by walking through the tree, discovering and assimilating information about the names. There should be two basic operations - to insert a new name or information into the symbol table as and when discovered and to efficiently lookup a name in the symbol table to retrieve its information.

Two common data structures used for the symbol table are -

1. Linear lists:- simple to implement, poor performance.

2. Hash tables:- greater programming/space overhead, good performance.

Ideally a compiler should be able to grow the symbol table dynamically, i.e., insert new entries or information as and when needed. But if the size of the table is fixed in advance then (an array implementation for example), then the size must be big enough in advance to accommodate the largest possible program.

Symbol Table Entries

- each entry for a declaration of a name

- format need not be uniform because information depends upon the usage of the name

- each entry is a record consisting of consecutive words

- to keep records uniform some entries may be outside the symbol table

- information is entered into symbol table at various times

  - keywords are entered initially

  - identifier lexemes are entered by lexical analyzer

- symbol table entry may be set up when role of name becomes clear

- attribute values are filled in as information is available

For each declaration of a name, there is an entry in the symbol table. Different entries need to store different information because of the different contexts in which a name can occur. An entry corresponding to a particular name can be inserted into the symbol table at different stages depending on when the role of the name becomes clear. The various attributes that an entry in the symbol table can have are lexeme, type of name, size of storage and in case of functions - the parameter list etc.

- a name may denote several objects in the same block

  - int x; struct x {float y, z; }

  - lexical analyzer returns the name itself and not pointer to symbol table entry

  - record in the symbol table is created when role of the name becomes clear

  - in this case two symbol table entries will be created

- attributes of a name are entered in response to declarations

- labels are often identified by colon

- syntax of procedure/function specifies that certain identifiers are formals

- characters in a name

  - there is a distinction between token id, lexeme and attributes of the names

  - it is difficult to work with lexemes

  - if there is modest upper bound on length then lexemes can be stored in symbol table

  - if limit is large store lexemes separately

There might be multiple entries in the symbol table for the same name, all of them having different roles. It is quite intuitive that the symbol table entries have to be made only when the role of a particular name becomes clear. The lexical analyzer therefore just returns the name and not the symbol table entry as it cannot determine the context of that name. Attributes corresponding to the symbol table are entered for a name in response to the corresponding declaration. There has to be an upper limit for the length of the lexemes for them to be stored in the symbol table.

Storage Allocation Information

- information about storage locations is kept in the symbol table

- if target is assembly code then assembler can take care of storage for various names

- compiler needs to generate data definitions to be appended to assembly code

- if target is machine code then compiler does the allocation

- for names whose storage is allocated at runtime no storage allocation is done

Information about the storage locations that will be bound to names at run time is kept in the symbol table. If the target is assembly code, the assembler can take care of storage for various names. All the compiler has to do is to scan the symbol table, after generating assembly code, and generate assembly language data definitions to be appended to the assembly language program for each name. If machine code is to be generated by the compiler, then the position of each data object relative to a fixed origin must be ascertained. The compiler has to do the allocation in this case. In the case of names whose storage is allocated on a stack or heap, the compiler does not allocate storage at all, it plans out the activation record for each procedure.

Data Structures

- List data structure

  - simplest to implement

  - use a single array to store names and information

  - search for a name is linear

  - entry and lookup are independent operations

  - cost of entry and search operations are very high and lot of time goes into book keeping

- Hash table

  - The advantages are obvious

Representing Scope Information

- entries are declarations of names

- when a lookup is done, entry for appropriate declaration must be returned

- scope rules determine which entry is appropriate

- maintain separate table for each scope

- symbol table for a procedure or scope is compile time equivalent an activation record

- information about non local is found by scanning symbol table for the enclosing procedures

- symbol table can be attached to abstract syntax of the procedure (integrated into intermediate representation)

The entries in the symbol table are for declaration of names. When an occurrence of a name in the source text is looked up in the symbol table, the entry for the appropriate declaration, according to the scoping rules of the language, must be returned. A simple approach is to maintain a separate symbol table for each scope.

- most closely nested scope rule can be implemented in data structures discussed so far

- give each procedure a unique number

- blocks must also be numbered

- procedure number is part of all local declarations

- name is represented as a pair of number and name

- names are entered in symbol table in the order they occur

- most closely nested rule can be created in terms of following operations:

  - lookup: find the most recently created entry

  - insert: make a new entry

  - delete: remove the most recently created entry

Most closely nested scope rules can be implemented by adapting the data structures. Each procedure is assigned a unique number. If the language is block-structured, the blocks must also be assigned unique numbers. The name is represented as a pair of a number and a name. This new name is added to the symbol table. Most scope rules can be implemented in terms of following operations:

a) Lookup - find the most recently created entry.

b) Insert - make a new entry.

c) Delete - remove the most recently created entry.

Symbol Table Structure

- Assign variables to storage classes that prescribe scope, visibility, and lifetime

- scope rules prescribe the symbol table structure

- scope: unit of static program structure with one or more variable declarations

- scope may be nested

- Pascal: procedures are scoping units

- C: blocks, functions, files are scoping units

- Visibility, lifetimes, global variables

- Common (in Fortran)

- Automatic or stack storage

- Static variables

storage class : A storage class is an extra keyword at the beginning of a declaration which modifies the declaration in some way. Generally, the storage class (if any) is the first word in the declaration, preceding the type name. Ex. static, extern etc.

Scope: The scope of a variable is simply the part of the program where it may be accessed or written. It is the part of the program where the variable's name may be used. If a variable is declared within a function, it is local to that function. Variables of the same name may be declared and used within other functions without any conflicts. For instance,

int fun1()

{

int a;

int b;

....

}

int fun2()

{

int a;

int c;

....

}

Visibility: The visibility of a variable determines how much of the rest of the program can access that variable. You can arrange that a variable is visible only within one part of one function, or in one function, or in one source file, or anywhere in the program

Local and Global variables: A variable declared within the braces {} of a function is visible only within that function; variables declared within functions are called *local variables*. On the other hand, a variable declared outside of any function is a *global variable* , and it is potentially visible anywhere within the program

Automatic Vs Static duration: How long do variables last? By default, local variables (those declared within a function) have *automatic duration* : they spring into existence when the function is called, and they (and their values) disappear when the function returns. Global variables, on the other hand, have *static duration* : they last, and the values stored in them persist, for as long as the program does. (Of course, the values can in general still be overwritten, so they don't necessarily persist forever.) By default, local variables have automatic duration. To give them static duration (so that, instead of coming and going as the function is called, they persist for as long as the function does), you precede their declaration with the static keyword: static int i; By default, a declaration of a global variable (especially if it specifies an initial value) is the defining instance. To make it an external declaration, of a variable which is defined somewhere else, you precede it with the keyword extern: extern int j; Finally, to arrange that a global variable is visible only within its containing source file, you precede it with the static keyword: static int k; Notice that the static keyword can do two different things: it adjusts the duration of a local variable from automatic to static, or it adjusts the visibility of a global variable from truly global to private-to-the-file.

Symbol Attributes and Symbol Table Entries

- Symbols have associated attributes

- typical attributes are name, type, scope, size, addressing mode etc.

- a symbol table entry collects together attributes such that they can be easily set and retrieved

- example of typical names in symbol table

Name	Type
name	character string
class	enumeration
size	integer
type	enumeration

Local Symbol Table Management

NewSymTab : SymTab ⟶ SymTab

DestSymTab : SymTab ⟶ SymTab

InsertSym : SymTab X Symbol ⟶ boolean

LocateSym : SymTab X Symbol ⟶ boolean

GetSymAttr : SymTab X Symbol X Attr ⟶ boolean

SetSymAttr : SymTab X Symbol X Attr X value ⟶ boolean

NextSym : SymTab X Symbol ⟶ Symbol

MoreSyms : SymTab X Symbol ⟶ boolean

These are prototypes of typical function declarations used for managing local symbol table. The right hand side of the arrows is the output of the procedure and the left side has the input.

- A major consideration in designing a symbol table is that insertion and retrieval should be as fast as possible

- One dimensional table: search is very slow

- Balanced binary tree: quick insertion, searching and retrieval; extra work required to keep the tree balanced

- Hash tables: quick insertion, searching and retrieval; extra work to compute hash keys

- Hashing with a chain of entries is generally a good approach

A major consideration in designing a symbol table is that insertion and retrieval should be as fast as possible. We talked about the one dimensional and hash tables a few slides back. Apart from these balanced binary trees can be used too. Hashing is the most common approach.

Hashed Local Symbol Table

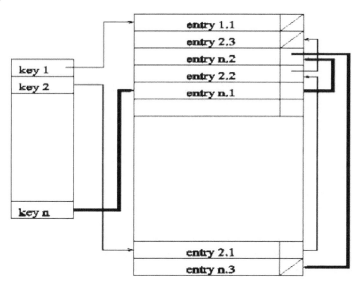

Hash tables can clearly implement 'lookup' and 'insert' operations. For implementing the 'delete', we do not want to scan the entire hash table looking for lists containing entries to be deleted. Each entry should have two links:

a) A hash link that chains the entry to other entries whose names hash to the same value - the usual link in the hash table.

b) A scope link that chains all entries in the same scope - an extra link. If the scope link is left undisturbed when an entry is deleted from the hash table, then the chain formed by the scope links will constitute an inactive symbol table for the scope in question.

Nesting Structure of an Example Pascal Program

```
program e;                              procedure i;
  var a, b, c: integer;                   var b, d: integer;
                                          begin
  procedure f;                              b:= a+c
    var a, b, c: integer;                 end;
    begin
      a := b+c                          procedure j;
    end;                                  var b, d: integer;
                                          begin
  procedure g;                              b := a+d
    var a, b: integer;                    end;

    procedure h;                        begin
      var c, d: integer;                  a := b+c
      begin                             end.
        c := a+d
      end;
```

Look at the nesting structure of this program. Variables a, b and c appear in global as well as local scopes. Local scope of a variable overrides the global scope of the other variable with the same name within its own scope. The local symbol tables for this structure. Here procedure I and h lie within the scope of g (are nested within g).

Global Symbol Table Structure

- scope and visibility rules determine the structure of global symbol table

- for Algol class of languages scoping rules structure the symbol table as tree of local tables

    - global scope as root

    - tables for nested scope as children of the table for the scope they are nested in

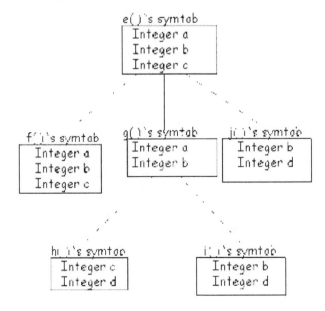

The global symbol table will be a collection of symbol tables connected with pointers. The exact structure will be determined by the scope and visibility rules of the language. Whenever a new scope is encountered a new symbol table is created. This new table contains a pointer back to the enclosing scope's symbol table and the enclosing one also contains a pointer to this new symbol table. Any variable used inside the new scope should either be present in its own symbol table or inside the enclosing scope's symbol table and all the way up to the root symbol table. A sample global symbol table is shown.

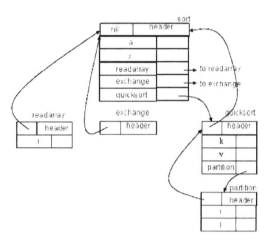

Another example.

Storage binding and symbolic registers

- Translates variable names into addresses
- This process must occur before or during code generation
- each variable is assigned an address or addressing method
- each variable is assigned an offset with respect to base which changes with every invocation
- variables fall in four classes: global, global static, stack, local (non-stack) static

The variable names have to be translated into addresses before or during code generation. There is a base address and every name is given an offset with respect to this base which changes with every invocation. The variables can be divided into four categories:

a) Global Variables

b) Global Static Variables

c) Stack Variables

d) Stack Static Variables

- global/static: fixed relocatable address or offset with respect to base as global pointer
- stack variable: offset from stack/frame pointer

- allocate stack/global in registers

- registers are not indexable, therefore, arrays cannot be in registers

- assign symbolic registers to scalar variables

- used for graph coloring for global register allocation

Global variables, on the other hand, have static duration (hence also called static variables): they last, and the values stored in them persist, for as long as the program does. (Of course, the values can in general still be overwritten, so they don't necessarily persist forever.) Therefore they have fixed relocatable address or offset with respect to base as global pointer. By default, local variables (stack variables) (those declared within a function) have automatic duration: they spring into existence when the function is called, and they (and their values) disappear when the function returns. This is why they are stored in stacks and have offset from stack/frame pointer. Register allocation is usually done for global variables. Since registers are not indexable, therefore, arrays cannot be in registers as they are indexed data structures. Graph coloring is a simple technique for allocating register and minimizing register spills that works well in practice. Register spills occur when a register is needed for a computation but all available registers are in use. The contents of one of the registers must be stored in memory to free it up for immediate use. We assign symbolic registers to scalar variables which are used in the graph coloring.

a: global   b: local   c[0..9]: local
gp: global pointer   fp: frame pointer

MIR	LIR	LIR
$a \leftarrow a{\cdot}2$	$r1 \leftarrow [gp+8]$	$s0 \leftarrow s0{\cdot}2$
	$r2 \leftarrow r1{\cdot}2$	
	$[gp+8] \leftarrow r2$	
$b \leftarrow a+c[1]$	$r3 \leftarrow [gp+8]$	$s1 \leftarrow [fp-28]$
	$r4 \leftarrow [fp-28]$	$s2 \leftarrow s0+s1$
	$r5 \leftarrow r3+r4$	
	$[fp-20] \leftarrow r5$	

Names bound
to symbolic
registers

Names bound
to locations

Local Variables in Frame

- assign to consecutive locations; allow enough space for each

  - may put word size object in half word boundaries

  - requires two half word loads

  - requires shift, or, and

- align on double word boundaries

  - wastes space

  - machine may allow small offsets

word boundaries - the most significant byte of the object must be located at an address whose two least significant bits are zero relative to the frame pointer

half-word boundaries - the most significant byte of the object being located at an address whose least significant bit is zero relative to the frame pointer

- sort variables by the alignment they need

- store largest variables first

  - automatically aligns all the variables

  - does not require padding

- store smallest variables first

  - requires more space (padding)

  - for large stack frame makes more variables accessible with small offsets

While allocating memory to the variables, sort variables by the alignment they need. You may:

- store largest variables first: It automatically aligns all the variables and does not require padding since the next variable's memory allocation starts at the end of that of the earlier variable

- store smallest variables first: It requires more space (padding) since you have to accommodate for the biggest possible length of any variable data structure. The advantage is that for large stack frame, more variables become accessible within small offsets

How to Store Large Local Data Structures

- Requires large space in local frames and therefore large offsets

- If large object is put near the boundary other objects require large offset either from fp (if put near beginning) or sp (if put near end)

- Allocate another base register to access large objects

- Allocate space in the middle or elsewhere; store pointer to these locations from at a small offset from fp

- Requires extra loads

Large local data structures require large space in local frames and therefore large offsets. If large objects are put near the boundary then the other objects require large offset. You can either allocate another base register to access large objects or you can allocate space in the middle or elsewhere and then store pointers to these locations starting from at a small offset from the frame pointer, fp.

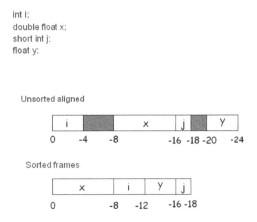

In the unsorted allocation you can see the waste of space in green. In sorted frame there is no waste of space.

Intermediate Code Generation

- Abstraction at the source level identifiers, operators, expressions, statements, conditionals, iteration, functions (user defined, system defined or libraries)

- Abstraction at the target level memory locations, registers, stack, opcodes, addressing modes, system libraries, interface to the operating systems

- Code generation is a mapping from source level abstractions to target machine abstractions

After syntax and semantic analysis, some compilers generate an explicit intermediate representation of the source program. We can think of this IR as a program for an abstract machine. This IR should have two important properties: It should be easy to produce and it should be easy to translate into target program. IR should have the abstraction in between of the abstraction at the source level (identifiers, operators, expressions, statements, conditionals, iteration, functions (user defined, system defined or libraries)) and of the abstraction at the target level (memory locations, registers, stack, opcodes, addressing modes, system libraries and interface to the operating systems). Therefore IR is an intermediate stage of the mapping from source level abstractions to target machine abstractions.

- Front end translates a source program into an intermediate representation

- Back end generates target code from intermediate representation

- Benefits

    - Retargeting is possible

    - Machine independent code optimization is possible

In the analysis-synthesis model of a compiler, the front end translates a source program into an intermediate representation from which the back end generates target code. Details of the target language are confined to the back end, as far as possible. Although a source program can be translated directly into the target language, some benefits of using a machine-independent intermediate form are:

1. Retargeting is facilitated: a compiler for a different machine can be created by attaching a back-end for the new machine to an existing front-end.

2. A machine-independent code optimizer can be applied to the intermediate representation.

Syntax Directed Translation of Expression into 3-address Code

S $\rightarrow$ id := E	S.code = E.code ||
	gen(id.place:= E.place)
E $\rightarrow$ E$_1$ + E$_2$	E.place:= newtmp
	E.code:= E$_1$.code || E$_2$.code ||
	gen(E.place := E$_1$.place + E$_2$.place)
E $\rightarrow$ E$_1$ * E$_2$	E.place:= newtmp
	E.code := E$_1$.code || E$_2$.code ||
	gen(E.place := E$_1$.place * E$_2$.place)

Three-address code is a sequence of statements of the general form

X := y op z

Where x, y and z are names, constants, or compiler generated temporaries. op stands for any operator, such as fixed- or floating-point arithmetic operator, or a logical operator on Boolean-valued data. Note that no built up arithmetic

expression are permitted, as there is only one operator on the right side of a statement. Thus a source language expression like x + y * z might be translated into a sequence

t1 := y * z

t2 := x + t1

where t1 and t2 are compiler-generated temporary names. This unraveling of complicated arithmetic expression and of nested flow-of-control statements makes three- address code desirable for target code generation and optimization.

The use of names for the intermediate values computed by a program allows three-address code to be easily rearranged unlike postfix notation. We can easily generate code for the three-address code given above. The S-attributed definition above generates three-address code for assigning statements. The synthesized attribute S.code represents the three-address code for the assignment S. The nonterminal E has two attributes:

- E.place , the name that will hold the value of E, and

- E.code , the sequence of three-address statements evaluating E.

The function newtemp returns a sequence of distinct names $t_1, t_2,..$ In response to successive calls.

$E \rightarrow -E_1$	E.place := newtmp
	E.code := E_1.code ||
	gen(E.place := - E_1.place)
$E \rightarrow (E_1)$	E.place := E_1.place
	E.code := E_1.code
$E \rightarrow id$	E.place := id.place
	E.code := ' '

Example

For a = b * -c + b * -c

following code is generated

$t_1 = -c$

$t_2 = b * t_1$

$t_3 = -c$

$t_4 = b * t_3$

$t_5 = t_2 + t_4$

$a = t_5$

$S \rightarrow$ while E do S_1	S.begin := newlabel
S. begin :	S.after := newlabel
E.code	
if E.place = 0 goto S.after	S.code := gen(S.begin:) ||
S_1.code	E.code ||
goto S.begin	gen(if E.place = 0 goto S.after) ||
S.after :	S_1.code ||
	gen(goto S.begin) ||
	gen(S.after:)

The syntax directed definition is shown. A new label S .*begin* is created and attached to the first instruction for E. Another new label S. *after* is created. The code for E generates a jump to the label if E is true, a jump to S.next if E is false; again, we set E.false to be S.next. After the code for S1 we place the instruction goto S.begin, which causes a jump back to the beginning of the code for the Boolean expression. Note that S1.next is set to this label S.begin, so jumps from within S1.code can directly to S.begin.

Flow of Control

S if E then S1 else S2	S.else := newlabel
	S.after := newlabel
E.code	
	S.code = E.code ||
if E.place = 0 goto S.else	gen(if E.place = 0 goto S.else) ||
S1 .code	S 1 .code ||
goto S.after	gen(goto S.after) ||
S.else:	gen(S.else :) ||
S 2 .code	gen(S.after :)
S.after:	

In translating the if-then-else statement the Boolean expression E jumps out of it to the first instruction of the code for S1 if E is true, and to first instruction of the code for S2 if E is false, as illustrated in the figure above. As with the if-then statement, an inherited attribute s.next gives the label of the three-address instruction to be executed next after executing the code for S. An explicit goto S.next appears after the code for S1, but not after S2.

Declarations

For each name create symbol table entry with information like type and relative address

P ⟶ {offset=0} D	
D ⟶ D ; D	
D ⟶ id : T	enter(id.name, T.type, offset);
	offset = offset + T.width
T ⟶ integer	T.type = integer; T.width = 4
T´ ⟶ real	T.type = real; T.width = 8

In the translation scheme nonterminal P generates a sequence of declarations of the form id : T . Before the first declaration is considered, offset is set to 0. As each new name is seen, that name is entered in the symbol table with the offset equal to the current value of offset, and offset is incremented by the width of the data object denoted by the name.

The procedure - enter (name, type, offset) creates a symbol-table entry for name , gives it type and relative address offset in its data area. We use synthesized attributes type and width for nonterminal T to indicate the type and Width, or number of memory units for nonterminal T to indicate the type and width, or number of memory units taken by objects of that type. If type expressions are represented by graphs, then attribute type might be a pointer to the node representing a type expression. We assume integers to have width of 4 and real to have width of 8. The width of an array is obtained by multiplying the width of each element by the number of elements in the array. The width of each pointer is also assumed to be 4.

$T \rightarrow$ array [num] of T_1

T.type = array(num.val, T_1.type)

T.width = num.val x T_1.width

$T \rightarrow \uparrow T_1$

T.type = pointer(T_1.type)

T.width = 4

Keeping Track of Local Information

- when a nested procedure is seen, processing of declaration in enclosing procedure is temporarily suspended

- assume following language $P \rightarrow D$ $D \rightarrow D$;D | id : T | proc id ;D ; S

- a new symbol table is created when procedure declaration $D \rightarrow$ proc id ; D1 ; S is seen

- entries for D1 are created in the new symbol table

- the name represented by id is local to the enclosing procedure

Until now, it has been discussed how declarations are processed when the language is such that it allows all the declarations in a procedure to be processed as a group. A single symbol table is used and a global variable offset is used to keep track of the next available relative address. In a language with nested procedures, names local to each procedure can be assigned relative addresses. Multiple symbol tables are used. When a procedure declaration is seen, processing of declarations in the enclosing procedure is temporarily suspended. Consider the following language:

P -> D

D -> D; D | id : T | proc id ; D ;S

Whenever a procedure declaration D proc id ; D1 ; S is processed, a new symbol table with a pointer to the symbol table of the enclosing procedure in its header is created and the entries for declarations in D1 are created in the new symbol table. The name represented by id is local to the enclosing procedure and is hence entered into the symbol table of the enclosing procedure.

Example

```
program sort;
    var a : array[1..n] of integer;
        x : integer;
    procedure readarray;
        var i : integer;

            ......
    procedure exchange(i,j:integers);

            ......
    procedure quicksort(m,n : integer);
        var k,v : integer;
            function partition(x,y:integer):integer;
                var i,j: integer;

                    ......

        ......
begin{main}
    ......
    end.
```

For the above procedures, entries for x, a and *quicksort* are created in the symbol table of *sort*. A pointer pointing to the symbol table of quicksort is also entered. Similarly, entries for k,v and partition are created in the symbol table of quicksort. The headers of the symbol tables of quicksort and partition have pointers pointing to sort and quicksort respectively

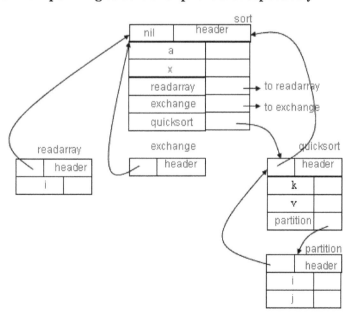

Creating Symbol Table

- mktable (previous)

create a new symbol table and return a pointer to the new table. The argument previous points to the enclosing procedure

- enter (table, name, type, offset)

creates a new entry

- addwidth (table, width)

records cumulative width of all the entries in a table

- enterproc (table, name, newtable)

creates a new entry for procedure name. newtable points to the symbol table of the new procedure

The following operations are designed :

1. mktable(previous): creates a new symbol table and returns a pointer to this table. *previous* is pointer to the symbol table of parent procedure.

2. enter(table,name,type,offset): creates a new entry for *name* in the symbol table pointed to by *table* .

3. addwidth(table,width): records cumulative width of entries of a table in its header.

4. enterproc(table,name ,newtable): creates an entry for procedure *name* in the symbol table pointed to by *table* . *newtable* is a pointer to symbol table for *name* .

P ⟶	{t=mktable(nil);
	push(t,tblptr);
	push(0,offset)}
D	
	{addwidth(top(tblptr),top(offset));
	pop(tblptr);
	pop(offset)}
D ⟶ D ;	D

The symbol tables are created using two stacks: *tblptr* to hold pointers to symbol tables of the enclosing procedures and offset whose top element is the next available relative address for a local of the current procedure. Declarations in nested procedures can be processed by the syntax directed definitions given below. Note that they are basically same as those given above but we have separately dealt with the epsilon productions. Go to the next page for the explanation.

```
P -> MD      {       addwidth(top(tblptr) ,top(offset));
                     pop(tblptr); pop(offset);
             }
M ->         {       t= mktable(nil);
                     push(t,tblptr);
                     push(0,offset);
             }
D -> D1 ; D2
D -> proc id ; ND1 ; S        {     t = top(tblptr);
                                    addwidth(t, top(offset));
                                    pop(tblptr); pop(offset);|
                                    enterproc(top(tblptr), id.name , t)
                              }
D -> id:T                     { enter (top(tblptr), id.name, T.type , top(offset));
                              top(offset) = top(offset) + T.width
                              }
N ->                          { t = mktable ( top(tblptr));
                              push(t,tblptr); push(0,offset);
                              }
```

$D \longrightarrow$ proc id;

    {t = mktable(top(tblptr));

    push(t, tblptr); push(0, offset)}

D 1 ; S

    {t = top(tblptr);

    addwidth(t, top(offset));

    pop(tblptr); pop(offset);;

    enterproc(top(tblptr), id.name, t)}

$D \longrightarrow$ id: T

    {enter(top(tblptr), id.name, T.type, top(offset));

    top(offset) = top (offset) + T.width}

The action for M creates a symbol table for the outermost scope and hence a nil pointer is passed in place of previous. When the declaration, D proc id ; ND1 ; S is processed, the action corresponding to N causes the creation of a symbol table for the procedure; the pointer to symbol table of enclosing procedure is given by top(tblptr). The pointer to the new table is pushed on to the stack tblptr and 0 is pushed as the initial offset on the offset stack. When the actions corresponding to the subtrees of N, D1 and S have been executed, the offset corresponding to the current procedure i.e., top(offset) contains the total width of entries in it. Hence top(offset) is added to the header of symbol table of the current procedure. The top entries of *tblptr* and *offset* are popped so that the pointer and offset of the enclosing procedure are now on top of these stacks. The entry for id is added to the symbol table of the enclosing procedure. When the declaration D -> id :T is processed entry for id is created in the symbol table of current procedure. Pointer to the symbol table of current procedure is again obtained from top(tblptr). Offset corresponding to the current procedure i.e. top(offset) is incremented by the width required by type T to point to the next available location.

Field Names in Records

T → record

  {t = mktable(nil);

  push(t, tblptr); push(0, offset)}

D end

  {T.type = record(top(tblptr));

  T.width = top(offset);

  pop(tblptr); pop(offset)}

T -> record LD end	{ t = mktable(nil); push(t, tblptr); push(0, offset) }
L ->	{ T.type = record(top(tblptr)); T.width = top(offset); pop(tblptr); pop(offset) }

The processing done corresponding to records is similar to that done for procedures. After the keyword record is seen the marker L creates a new symbol table. Pointer to this table and offset o are pushed on the respective stacks. The action for the declaration D -> id :T push the information about the field names on the table created. At the end the top of the offset stack contains the total width of the data objects within the record. This is stored in the attribute T.width. The constructor *record* is applied to the pointer to the symbol table to obtain T.type.

Names in the Symbol Table

S → id := E

  {p = lookup(id.place);

  if p <> nil then emit(p := E.place)

    else error}

E → id

  {p = lookup(id.name);

  if p <> nil then E.place = p

    else error}

The operation *lookup* in the translation scheme above checks if there is an entry for this occurrence of the name in the symbol table. If an entry is found, pointer to the entry is returned else nil is returned. *lookup* first checks whether the name appears in the current symbol table. If not then it looks for the name in the symbol table of the enclosing procedure and so on. The pointer to the symbol table of the enclosing procedure is obtained from the header of the symbol table.

Addressing Array Elements

- Arrays are stored in a block of consecutive locations

- assume width of each element is w

- ith element of array A begins in location base + (i - low) x w where base is relative address of A[low]

- the expression is equivalent to

i x w + (base-low x w)

$\longrightarrow$ i x w + const

Elements of an array are stored in a block of consecutive locations. For a single dimensional array, if low is the lower bound of the index and base is the relative address of the storage allocated to the array i.e., the relative address of A[low], then the i th Elements of an array are stored in a block of consecutive locations.

For a single dimensional array, if low is the lower bound of the index and base is the relative address of the storage allocated to the array i.e., the relative address of A[low], then the i th elements begins at the location: base + (I - low)* w . This expression can be reorganized as i*w + (base -low*w) . The sub-expression base-low*w is calculated and stored in the symbol table at compile time when the array declaration is processed, so that the relative address of A[i] can be obtained by just adding i*w to it.

2-dimensional Array

- storage can be either row major or column major

- in case of 2-D array stored in row major form address of $A[i_1, i_2]$ can be calculated as

  base + ((i_1 - low_1) x n_2 + i_2 - low_2) x w

where n_2 = $high_2$ - low_2 + 1

- rewriting the expression gives

  ((i_1 x n_2) + i_2) x w + (base - ((low_1 x n_2) + low_2) x w)

  $\longrightarrow$ ((i_1 x n_2) + i_2) x w + constant

- this can be generalized for $A[i_1, i_2, .., i_k]$

Similarly, for a row major two dimensional array the address of A[i][j] can be calculated by the formula :

base + ((i-low$_i$)*n2 +j - low$_j$)*w where low$_i$ and low$_j$ are lower values of I and j and n2 is number of values j can take i.e. n2 = high2 - low2 + 1.

This can again be written as :

((i * n2) + j) *w + (base - ((low$_i$ *n2) + low$_j$) * w) and the second term can be calculated at compile time.

In the same manner, the expression for the location of an element in column major two-dimensional array can be obtained. This addressing can be generalized to multidimensional arrays.

Example

- Let A be a 10x20 array therefore, n 1 = 10 and n 2 = 20 and assume w = 4
- code to access A[y,z] is

$t_1 = y * 20$

$t_1 = t_1 + z$

$t_2 = 4 * t_1$

$t_3 = A-84 \{((low_1 Xn_2)+low_2)Xw)=(1*20+1)*4=84\}$

$t_4 = t_2 + t_3$

$x = t_4$

Let A be a 10x20 array

n1 = 10 and n2 = 20

Assume width of the type stored in the array is 4. The three address code to access A[y,z] is

t1 = y * 20

t1 = t1 + z

t2 = 4 *t1

t3 =base A -84 {((low 1 *n2)+low 2)*w)=(1*20+1)*4=84}

t4 =t2 +t3

x = t4

Type Conversion within Assignments

$E \rightarrow E_1 + E_2$

E.place= newtmp;

if E_1 .type = integer and E_2 .type = integer

then emit(E.place ':=' E_1 .place 'int+' E_2 .place);

E.type = integer;

.

similar code if both E_1 .type and E_2 .type are real

.

else if E_1 .type = int and E_2 .type = real

then

u = newtmp;

emit(u ':=' inttoreal E_1 .place);

emit(E.place ':=' u 'real+' E_2 .place);

E.type = real;

.

similar code if E_1 .type is real and E_2 .type is integer

When a compiler encounters mixed type operations it either rejects certain mixed type operations or generates coercion instructions for them.

Semantic action for E -> E1+ E2:

E.place= newtmp;

if E1.type = integer and E2.type = integer

then emit(E.place ':=' E1.place 'int+' E2.place);

E.type = integer;

..

similar code if both E1.type and E2.type are real

.

else if E1.type = int and E2.type = real

then

u = newtmp;

emit(u ':=' inttoreal E1.place);

emit(E.place ':=' u 'real+' E2.place);

E.type = real;

.

similar code if E1.type is real and E2.type is integer

The three address statement of the form u ':=' inttoreal E1.place denotes conversion of an integer to real. int+ denotes integer addition and real+ denotes real addition.

Code generation is done along with type checking and if type resolution can be done in a single pass no intermediate representation like an abstract syntax tree would be required.

Example

real x, y;

int i, j;

x = y + i * j

generates code

t1 = i int* j

t2 = inttoreal t 1

t3 = y real+ t 2

x = t 3

Here is an example of type conversion within assignments

Boolean Expressions

- compute logical values

- change the flow of control

- boolean operators are: and or not

$$
\begin{aligned}
E \to\ & E \text{ or } E \\
|\ & E \text{ and } E \\
|\ & \text{not } E \\
|\ & (E) \\
|\ & id \text{ relop } id \\
|\ & true \\
|\ & false
\end{aligned}
$$

Boolean expressions are used to compute logical values and as conditional expressions in statements that alter flow of control such as if-then statements. Boolean expressions are composed of the Boolean operators and, or, not - applied to boolean variables or relational expressions.

Relational expressions are of the form E1 relop E2 where E1 and E2 are arithmetic expressions. Boolean expressions can be generated by the following grammar-

E -> E or E | E and E | not E | (E) | id relop id | true | false

Methods of Translation

- Evaluate similar to arithmetic expressions

  - Normally use 1 for true and 0 for false

- implement by flow of control

  - given expression E_1 or E_2 if E_1 evaluates to true then E_1 or E_2 evaluates to true without evaluating E_2

There are two principal methods of representing the value of Boolean expressions-

1. Encode true and false numerically and evaluate analogously to an arithmetic expression. Normally 1 is used to denote true and 0 to denote false.

2. Implementing Boolean expressions by flow of control, that is, representing the value of a Boolean expression by the position reached in the program. For example, consider the expression - a or (b and c). If the value of a is true the values of b and c can be ignored and the entire expression can be assigned the value true. If a is false the value of (b and c) needs to be considered. If the value of b is false, the expression (b and c) and hence the entire expression can be assigned value false. The value of c needs to be considered only if a is false and b is true.

Numerical Representation

- a or b and not c

t_1 = not c

t_2 = b and t_1

t_3 = a or t_2

- relational expression a < b is equivalent to if a < b then 1 else 0

1. if a < b goto 4.

2. t = 0

3. goto 5

4. t = 1

Consider the implementation of Boolean expressions using 1 to denote true and 0 to denote false. Expressions are evaluated in a manner similar to arithmetic expressions.

For example, the three address code for a or b and not c is:

t1 = not c

t2 = b and t1

t3 = a or t2

Syntax Directed Translation of Boolean Expressions

$E \longrightarrow E_1$ or E_2

      E.place := newtmp

      emit(E.place ':=' E_1 .place ‹or› E_2 .place)

$E \longrightarrow E_1$ and E_2

      E.place:= newtmp

      emit(E.place ':=' E_1 .place ‹and› E_2 .place)

$E \longrightarrow$ not E_1

      E.place := newtmp

      emit(E.place ':=' 'not' E_1 .place)

$E \longrightarrow (E_1)$ E.place = E_1 .place

$E \longrightarrow$ id1 relop id2

      E.place := newtmp

      emit(if id1.place relop id2.place goto nextstat+3)

      emit(E.place = 0) emit(goto nextstat+2)

      emit(E.place = 1)

$E \longrightarrow$ true

      E.place := newtmp

      emit(E.place = '1')

$E \longrightarrow$ false

      E.place := newtmp

      emit(E.place = '0')

In the above scheme, nextstat gives the index of the next three address code in the output sequence and emit increments nextstat after producing each three address statement.

Example: Code for a < b or c < d and e < f

100: if a < b goto 103	if e < f goto 111
101: t_1 = 0	109: t_3 = 0
102: goto 104	110: goto 112
103: t_1 = 1	111: t_3 = 1
104:	112:
if c < d goto 107	t_4 = t_2 and t_3
105: t_2 = 0	113: t_5 = t_1 or t_4
106: goto 108	
107: t_2 = 1	
108:	

A relational expression a < b is equivalent to the conditional statement if a < b then 1 else 0 and three address code for this expression is:

100: if a < b goto 103.

101: t = 0

102: goto 104

103: t = 1

104:

It is continued from 104 in the same manner as the above written block.

Short Circuit Evaluation of boolean expressions

- Translate boolean expressions without:
    - generating code for boolean operators
    - evaluating the entire expression
- Flow of control statements

    S if E then S1

    | if E then S1 else S 2

    | while E do S 1

We can translate a boolean expression into three-address code without generating code for boolean operators and without evaluating the entire expression. Take the case of the previous example, here we can tell the value of t by whether we reach statement 101 or 103, so the value of t becomes redundant. Similarly, for larger expressions the value can be determined without having to evaluate the expression completely. However, if a part of the expression having a side effect is not evaluated, the side effect will not be visible.

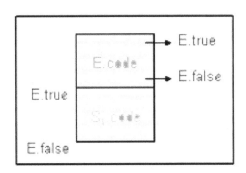

S ? if E then S 1

        E.true = newlabel

        E.false = S.next

        S1 .next = S.next

        S.code = E.code ||

                gen(E.true ':') ||

                S1 .code

Now we will consider the translation of boolean expressions into three address code generated by the following grammar:

S -> if E then S1

        | if E then S1 else S2

        | while E do S1

where E is the boolean expression to be translated.

Consider the following:

newlabel - returns a new symbolic label each time it is called.

E.true - the label to which control flows if E is true.

E.false - the label to which control flows if E is false.

For if-then

S -> if E then S1

E.true = newlabel   //generate a new label for E.true

E.false = S.next   //jump to S.next if E is false

S1.next = S.next

S.code = E.code || gen(E.true ':') || S1.code   // associate the label created for E.true with the

             // three address code for the first statement for S1

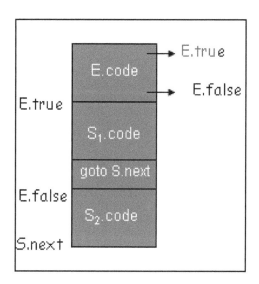

S ⟶ if E then S1 else S2
E.true = newlabel
E.false = newlabel
S 1 .next = S.next
S2 .next = S.next
S.code = E.code ||

gen(E.true ':') ||
S 1 .code ||
gen(goto S.next) ||
gen(E.false ':') ||
S 2 .code

For *if-then-else*

S -> if E then S1 else S2

E.true = newlabel

E.false = newlabel

S1.next = S.next

S2.next = S.next

S.code = E.code || gen(E.true ':') || S1.code || gen('goto' S.next) || gen(E.false ':') || S2.code

In the above code, the labels E.true and E.false created are associated with the first three address code instructions for S1 and S2 respectively, so that if E is true, jump to S1 occurs and if E is false jump to S2 occurs. An explicit goto S.next is required after the code of S1 to ensure that after execution of code for S1 control moves to the statement after S instead of falling through the code of S2, in case E is true.

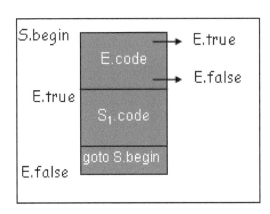

$S \longrightarrow$ while E do S 1

S.begin = newlabel

E.true = newlabel

E.false = S.next

S 1 .next = S.begin

S.ocde = gen(S.begin ':') ||

E.code ||

gen(E.true ':') ||

S 1 .code ||

gen(goto S.begin)

For *while-do*

S -> while E do S1

S.begin = newlabel

E.true = newlabel

E.false = S.next

S1.next = S.begin

S.code = gen(S.begin ':') || E.code || gen(E.true ':') || S1.code || gen(goto S.begin)

In case of while-do statement a new label S.begin is created and associated with the first instruction of the code for E, so that control can be transferred back to E after the execution of S1. E.false is set to S.next, so that control moves out of the code for S in case E is false. Since S1.next is set to S.begin, jumps from the code for S1 can go directly to S.begin.

Control Flow Translation of Boolean Expression

E E1 or E 2   E1 .true := E.true

E 1 .false := newlabel

E2 .true := E.true

E2 .false := E.false

E.code := E 1 .code || gen(E 1 .false) || E2 .code

E E 1 and E2   E 1 .true := new label

E 1 false := E.false

E2 .true := E.true

E2 false := E.false

E.code := E 1 .code || gen(E1 .true) || E2 .code

E is translated into a sequence of conditional and unconditional jumps to one of the two locations: E.true or E.false depending if E is true or false.

If E is of the form E1 or E2, then if E1 is true then we immediately know that E itself is true, so E1.true is the same as E.true. If E1 is false then E2 must be evaluated, so E1.false is the label of the first statement of E2. If E2 is evaluated and E2 is true, it implies that E is true, so E2.true is set to E.true. Similarly, if E2 is evaluated and it is false, the entire expression is false.

E -> E1 or E2 E1.true := E.true

E1.false := newlabel

E2.true := E.true

E2.false := E.false

E.code := E1.code || gen(E1.false) || E2.code

Analogously E1 and E2 can also be translated. Here if E1 is false then there need be no further considerations.

E -> E1 and E2 E1.true := new label

E1 false := E.false

E2.true := E.true

E2 false := E.false

E.code := E1.code || gen(E1.true) || E2.code

$E \rightarrow$ not E_1	E_1 .true := E.false
	E_1 .false := E.true
	E.code := E_1 .code
$E \rightarrow (E_1)$	E_1 .true := E.true
	E_1 .false := E.false
	E.code := E_1 .code

For an expression E of the form *not* E1, just interchange the true and false exits of E1 to get the true and false exits of E.

E -> not E1 E1.true := E.false

E1.false := E.true

E.code := E1.code

If E is a bracketed expression, it means the same as E1 and so E1.false and E1.true are set to E.false and E.true respectively.

E -> (E1) E1.true := E.true

E1.false := E.false

E.code := E1.code

if E is of the form

a < b

then code is of the form

if a < b goto E.true

goto E.false

$E \to id_1 \ relop \ id_2$

E.code = gen(if id_1 relop id_2 goto E.true) ||
gen(goto E.false)

$E \to true$ E.code = gen(goto E.true)

$E \to false$ E.code = gen(goto E.false)

if E is of the form a < b then the generated code is of the form:

if a < b goto E.true

goto E.false

E -> id1 relop id2 E.code = gen(if id1 relop id2 goto E.true) ||gen(goto E.false)

E -> true E.code= gen(goto E.true)

E -> false E.code= gen(goto E.false)

Example

Code for a < b or c < d and e < f

if a < b goto Ltrue

goto L1

L1: if c < d goto L2

goto Lfalse

L2: if e < f goto Ltrue

goto Lfalse

Ltrue:

Lfalse:

Code for a < b or c < d and e < f

It is equivalent to a<b or (c<d and e<f) by precedence of operators.

Code:

>   if a < b goto L.true

>   goto L1

L1 : if c < d goto L2

>   goto L.false

L2 : if e < f goto L.true

>   goto L.false

where L.true and L.false are the true and false exits for the entire expression.

(The code generated is not optimal as the second statement can be eliminated without changing the value of the code).

Code for while a < b do

>   if c < d then

>> x = y + z

>   else

>> x = y - z

```
        Code for              while a < b do
                                if c<d then
                                    x=y+z
                              else
                                    x=y-z

        L1:    if a < b goto L2
               goto Lnext
        L2:    if c < d goto L3
               goto L4
        L3:    t₁ = Y + Z
               X= t₁
               goto L1
        L4:    t₁ = Y - Z
               X= t₁
               goto LI
        Lnext:
```

L1 : if a < b goto L2   //no jump to L2 if a>=b. next instruction causes jump outside the loop

      goto L.next

L2 : if c < d goto L3

      goto L4

L3 : t1 = Y + Z

      X= t1

      goto L1   //return to the expression code for the while loop

L4 : t1 = Y - Z

      X= t1

      goto L1   //return to the expression code for the while loop

L.next:

Here too the first two goto statements can be eliminated by changing the direction of the tests (by translating a relational expression of the form id1 < id2 into the statement if id1 id2 goto E.false).

Case Statement

- switch expression

begin

      case value: statement

      case value: statement

..

      case value: statement

      default: statement

end

- evaluate the expression
- find which value in the list of cases is the same as the value of the expression
  - Default value matches the expression if none of the values explicitly mentioned in the cases matches the expression
- execute the statement associated with the value found

There is a selector expression, which is to be evaluated, followed by n constant values that the expression can take. This may also include a *default* value which always matches the expression if no other value does. The intended translation of a switch case code to:

- evaluate the expression

- find which value in the list of cases is the same as the value of the expression.

- Default value matches the expression if none of the values explicitly mentioned in the cases matches the expression . execute the statement associated with the value found

Most machines provide instruction in hardware such that case instruction can be implemented easily. So, case is treated differently and not as a combination of if-then statements.

Translation

code to evaluate E into t	code to evaluate E into t
if t <> V1 goto L1	goto test
code for S1	L1: code for S1
goto next	goto next
L1 if t <> V2 goto L2	L2: code for S2
code for S2	goto next
goto next	..
L2: ..	Ln: code for Sn
Ln-2 if t <> Vn-l goto Ln-l	goto next
code for Sn-l	test: if t = V1 goto L1
goto next	if t = V2 goto L2
Ln-1: code for Sn	..
next:	if t = Vn-1 goto Ln-1
	goto Ln
	next:

Efficient for N-way Branch

There are two ways of implementing switch-case statements, both given above. The above two implementations are equivalent except that in the first case all the jumps are short jumps while in the second case they are long jumps. However, many machines provide the n-way branch which is a hardware instruction. Exploiting this instruction is much easier in the second implementation while it is almost impossible in the first one. So, if hardware has this instruction the second method is much more efficient.

BackPatching

- way to implement boolean expressions and flow of control statements in one pass

- code is generated as quadruples into an array

- labels are indices into this array

- makelist(i): create a newlist containing only i, return a pointer to the list.

- merge(p1,p2): merge lists pointed to by p1 and p2 and return a pointer to the concatenated list

- backpatch(p,i): insert i as the target label for the statements in the list pointed to by p

Backpatching is a technique to solve the problem of replacing symbolic names in goto statements by the actual target addresses. This problem comes up because of some languages do not allow symbolic names in the branches. Idea: Maintain a list of branches that have the same target label (the function backpatch(p,i) does this only) and replace them once they are defined.

Backpatching can be summarized as this:

- Two-pass implementation: (1) syntax tree (2) depth-first walk
- back-patching (one-pass)
- construct the syntax tree
- depth-first order tree walk computing translations
- generate jumps with unspecified targets (labels)
- keep a list of such statements
- subsequently fill in the labels (back-patching)
- implementation + operations
- table of quadruples; labels as indexes into this table
- makelist(i) create a new list containing only i
- merge(p1, p2) concatenate lists and return pointer
- backpatch(p, i) insert i as a target label for each of statements on list with pointer p

Boolean Expressions

$E \longrightarrow E_1$ or M E_2

$\mid E_1$ and M E_2

$\mid$ not E_1

$\mid (E_1)$

$\mid id_1$ relop id_2

$\mid$ true

$\mid$ false M ? ε

- Insert a marker non terminal M into the grammar to pick up index of next quadruple.
- attributes truelist and falselist are used to generate jump code for boolean expressions
- incomplete jumps are placed on lists pointed to by E.truelist and E.falselist

E.truelist and E.falselist have just incomplete jumps as of now. The entries in this list will be given targets (subsequent filling of labels) later on - backpatching.

- Consider $E \longrightarrow E_1$ and M E_2

- if E_1 is false then E is also false so statements in E_1.falselist become part of E.falselist

- if E_1 is true then E_2 must be tested so target of E_1.truelist is beginning of E_2

- target is obtained by marker M

- attribute M.quad records the number of the first statement of E_2.code

truelist and faliselist are synthesized attributes. if E_1 is false then E is also false so statements in E_1.falselist become part of E.falselist. And if E_1 is true then E_2 must be tested so target of E_1.truelist is beginning of E_2. The target of E_1.truelist is obtained from the marker M with the help of M.quad which records the number (position) of the first statement of E_2.code because if E_1 is true then the code flow will depend on E_2.

$E \longrightarrow E_1$ or M E_2

      backpatch(E_1.falselist, M.quad)

      E.truelist = merge(E_1.truelist, E_2.truelist)

      E.falselist = E_2.falselist

$E \longrightarrow E_1$ and M E_2

      backpatch(E_1.truelist, M.quad)

      E.truelist = E_2.truelist

      E.falselist = merge(E_1.falselist, E_2.falselist)

$E \longrightarrow$ not E_1

      E.truelist = E_1 falselist

      E.falselist = E_1.truelist

$E \longrightarrow (E_1)$

      E.truelist = E_1.truelist

      E.falselist = E_1.falselist

This is the backpatching translation scheme.

$E \longrightarrow E_1$ or M E_2

In this case

- if E1 is false then E2 will be looked into. Hence backpatch(E_1.falselist, M.quad)

- If one of E1 or E2 is true then E is true, hence E.truelist = merge(E_1.truelist, E_2.truelist)

- If E2 is checked then E1 must have been found to be false, hence Es falselist will be same as E1s falselist. Hence E.falselist = E_2.falselist

$E \rightarrow E_1$ and M E_2

- In this case if E1 is true then E2 will be looked into. Hence backpatch(E_1 .truelist, M.quad)

- If one of E1 or E2 is false then E is false, hence E.falselist = merge(E_1 .falselist, E_2 .falselist)

- If E2 checked then E1 must have been found to be true, hence Es truelist will be same as E2s truelist. Hence E.truelist = E_2 .truelist

Similarly we can conclude for other two cases given above.

$E \rightarrow$ id 1 relop id 2

 E.truelist = makelist(nextquad)

 E.falselist = makelist(nextquad+ 1)

 emit(if id 1 relop id 2 goto ---)

 emit(goto ---)

$E \rightarrow$ true

 E.truelist = makelist(nextquad)

 emit(goto ---)

$E \rightarrow$ false

 E.falselist = makelist(nextquad)

 emit(goto ---)

$M \rightarrow \varepsilon$

 M.quad = nextquad

Generate Code for a < b or c < d and e < f

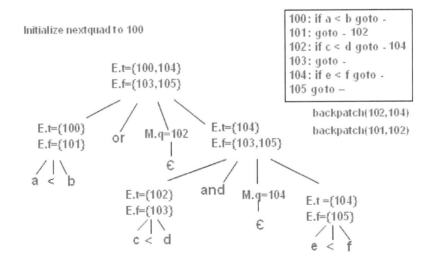

We finally get the values of E.t and E.f by bottom up evaluation of the tree.

from E => E_1 or M E_2

{ backpatch(E_1 .falselist, M.quad); ...}

=>

{ backpatch({101}, 102); ...}

gives 101: goto 102

from E => E_1 and M E_2

{ backpatch(E_1 .truelist, M.quad); ...}

=>

{ backpatch({102}, 104); ...} gives

102: if c < d goto 104

Note that:

- the entire expression is true if the gotos of statements 100 or 104 are reached,

- the entire expression is false if the gotos of statements 103 or 105 are reached, and

- these targets will be filled in later when the action depending on the true/false is known.

Flow of Control Statements

S $\longrightarrow$ if E then S 1

      | if E then S 1 else S 2

      | while E do S 1

      | begin L end

      | A

L $\longrightarrow$ L ; S

      | S

      S : Statement

      A : Assignment

      L : Statement list

The above given example has these flow of control statements of the backpatching grammar. We will attach rules to each reduction for the backpatching.

Scheme to Implement Translation

- E has attributes truelist and falselist

- L and S have a list of unfilled quadruples to be filled by backpatching

- $S \longrightarrow$ while E do S_1 requires labels S.begin and E.true

  - markers M_1 and M_2 record these labels $S \longrightarrow$ while $M_1 E$ do $M_2 S_1$

  - when while. .. is reduced to S backpatch S_1.nextlist to make target of all the statements to

M_1.quad

  - E.truelist is backpatched to go to the beginning of S_1 (M_2.quad)

E has attributes truelist and falselist. L and S have a list of unfilled quadruples to be filled by back-patching.

For example consider $S \longrightarrow$ while E do S_1

M_1 and M_2 are used to record the quad numbers of S.begin and E.true respectively. B ackpatching is used to ensure that all targets on S_1. nextlist are M_1.quad. E.truelist is back-patched to go to the beginning of S_1 by making jumps on E.truelist targeted towards M_2.quad. A n explicit jump to the beginning of the code for E is appended after the code for S_1 to prevent control from «falling out the bottom».

$S \longrightarrow$ if E then M S_1

     backpatch(E.truelist, M.quad)

     S.nextlist = merge(E.falselist, S_1 .nextlist)

$S \longrightarrow$ if E them $M_1 S_1 N$ else $M_2 S_2$

     backpatch(E.truelist, M_1 .quad)

     backpatch(E.falselist, M_2 .quad)

     S.next = merge(S_1 .nextlist, N.nextlist, S_2 .nextlist

$S \longrightarrow$ while $M_1 E$ do $M_2 S_1$

     backpatch(S_1 .nextlist, M_1 .quad)

     backpatch(E.truelist, M_2 .quad)

     S.nextlist = E.falselist

     emit(goto M_1 .quad)

We explained the rules for $S \longrightarrow$ while $M_1 E$ do $M_2 S_1$. Now you can see the rules for all the other statements and you can infer them quite easily on similar grounds.

S ⟶ begin L end	S.nextlist = L.nextlist
S ⟶ A	S.nextlist = makelist()
L ⟶ L1 ; M S	backpatch(L1 .nextlist, M.quad)
	L.nextlist = S.nextlist
L ⟶ S	L.nextlist = S.nextlist
N ⟶ ε	N.nextlist = makelist(nextquad)
	emit(goto ---)
M ⟶ ε	M.quad = nextquad

Procedure Calls

S ⟶ call id (Elist)

Elist ⟶ Elist , E

Elist ⟶ E

- Calling sequence

    - allocate space for activation record

    - evaluate arguments

    - establish environment pointers

    - save status and return address

    - jump to the beginning of the procedure

calling sequences

- allocate space for activation record (AR) on stack

- evaluate arguments to procedure and make available at known location

- save state of calling procedure - used to resume execution after call

- save return address (in known location) (instruction following call)

- generate jump to the beginning of the called procedure

return sequence

- if a function, save the result(s) in a known place

- restore the activation record of the calling procedure

- generate a jump to the return address (of calling procedure)

Example

- parameters are passed by reference

- storage is statically allocated

- use param statement as place holder for the arguments

- called procedure is passed a pointer to the first parameter

- pointers to any argument can be obtained by using proper offsets

The parameters are passed by reference and have statically allocated storage.

Code Generation

- Generate three address code needed to evaluate arguments which are expressions

- Generate a list of param three address statements

- Store arguments in a list

S ⟶ call id (Elist)

    for each item p on queue do emit('param' p)

    emit('call' id.place)

Elist ⟶ Elist , E

    append E.place to the end of queue

Elist ⟶ E

    initialize queue to contain E.place

For code generation, we generate three address code which is needed to evaluate arguments that are in fact expressions. As a result a list of param three address statements are generated. This is a syntax-directed translation and gives: param p_1 ; param p_2 ; param p_n ; call id.place Note that each of the expression will also generate 3ac code

References

- "An ILOC Simulator" by W. A. Barrett 2007, paraphrasing Keith Cooper and Linda Torczon, "Engineering a Compiler", Morgan Kaufmann, 2004. ISBN 1-55860-698-X

- FDA (2010-09-08). "Infusion Pump Software Safety Research at FDA". Food and Drug Administration. Retrieved 2010-09-09

- Wichmann, B. A.; Canning, A. A.; Clutterbuck, D. L.; Winsbarrow, L. A.; Ward, N. J.; Marsh, D. W. R. (Mar 1995). "Industrial Perspective on Static Analysis." (PDF). Software Engineering Journal: 69–75. Archived from the original (PDF) on 2011-09-27

- VDC Research (2012-02-01). "Automated Defect Prevention for Embedded Software Quality". VDC Research. Retrieved 2012-04-10

- M. Howard and S. Lipner. The Security Development Lifecycle: SDL: A Process for Developing Demonstrably More Secure Software. Microsoft Press, 2006. ISBN 978-0735622142

- Chow, Fred (2013-11-22). "The Challenge of Cross-language Interoperability". ACM Queue. 11 (10). Retrieved 2016-02-12

- Vijay D'Silva; et al. (2008). "A Survey of Automated Techniques for Formal Software Verification" (PDF). Transactions On CAD. Retrieved 2015-05-11

- Jones, Paul (2010-02-09). "A Formal Methods-based verification approach to medical device software analysis". Embedded Systems Design. Archived from the original on July 10, 2011. Retrieved 2010-09-09

Runtime System: An Overview

Runtime system, like compiler, is a part of program execution. It is required to manage the sequence of work that gets performed, which is listed through programming language. It acts as a gateway between the running program and the runtime environment. The chapter closely examines the key concepts of compiler design to provide an extensive understanding of the subject.

Runtime System

A runtime system, also called run-time system, primarily implements portions of an execution model. This is in contrast to the runtime lifecycle phase of a program, during which the runtime system is in operation. Most languages have some form of runtime system, which implements control over the order in which work that was specified in terms of the language gets performed. Over the years, the meaning of the term 'runtime system' has been expanded to include nearly any behaviors that are dynamically determined during execution.

Overview

Every programming language specifies an execution model, and many implement at least part of that model in a runtime system. One, debatable, way to define a runtime system is that any behavior that is not directly the work of a program is runtime system behavior. This definition includes as part of the runtime system things such as putting parameters onto the stack before a function call, the behavior of disk I/O, and parallel execution related behaviors.

By this definition, essentially every language has a runtime system, including compiled languages, interpreted languages, and embedded domain-specific languages. Even API invoked stand alone execution models such as Pthreads have a runtime system that is the implementation of execution model's behavior.

Most scholarly papers on runtime systems focus on the implementation details of parallel runtime systems. A notable example of a parallel runtime system is that of Cilk, a popular parallel programming model. In addition, the proto-runtime toolkit was created to simplify the creation of parallel runtime systems.

In addition to the execution model behavior, a runtime system may also perform support services such as type checking, debugging, or code generation and optimization.

The runtime system is also the gateway by which a running program interacts with the runtime environment, which contains not only state values that are accessible during program execution, but also active entities that can be interacted with during program execution like disk drives and people, via keyboards. For example, environment variables are features of many operating systems, and are part of the runtime environment; a running program can access them via the runtime system. Likewise, hardware devices such as a DVD drive are active entities that a program can interact with via a runtime system.

A unique application of a runtime environment (RTE) is within an operating system (OS) that *only* allows that RTE to run, meaning from boot until power-down the entire OS is dedicated to only the application(s) running within that RTE. Any other code that tries to run or any failures in the application(s) break the RTE which breaks the OS which stops all processing and requires a reboot. If the boot is from read-only memory, an extremely secure, simple, single-mission system is created. For example, this an easy way to create a never-needs-patching, can-never-be-modified Internet of Things device. In this case, the IOT could not be used for other purposes (e.g. a botnet) but nor can it be patched to prevent exploiting vulnerabilities to force a reboot.

Examples

As a simple example of a basic runtime system, the runtime system of the C language is a particular set of instructions inserted into the executable image by the compiler. Among other things, these instructions manage the processor stack, create space for local variables, and copy function-call parameters onto the top of the stack. There are often no clear criteria for deciding which language behavior is considered inside the runtime system versus which behavior is "compiled". In this case, the reason that C's stack behavior is part of the runtime system, as opposed to part of a keyword of the language, is that it is systematic, maintaining the state of the stack throughout a program's execution. The systematic behavior implements the execution model of the language, as opposed to implementing semantics of particular keywords which are directly translated into code that computes results.

Another example, which illuminates the nature of a runtime system, is the case of using an application programming interface (API) to interact with a runtime system. The calls to that API look the same as calls to a regular software library, however at some point during the call the execution model changes. The runtime system implements an execution model different from that of the language the library is written in terms of. A person reading the code of a normal library would be able to understand the library's behavior by just knowing the language the library was written in. However, a person reading the code of the API that invokes a runtime system would not be able to understand the behavior of the API call just by knowing the language the call was written in. At some point, via some mechanism, the execution model stops being that of the language the call is written in and switches over to being the execution model implemented by the runtime system. For example, the trap instruction is one method of switching execution models. This difference is what distinguishes an API-invoked execution model, such as POSIX threads, from a usual software library. Both POSIX threads calls and software library calls are invoked via an API, but POSIX threads behavior cannot be understood in terms of the language of the call. Rather, POSIX threads calls bring into play an outside execution model, which is implemented by the POSIX threads runtime system (this runtime system is often the OS kernel).

Advanced Features

Some compiled or interpreted languages provide an interface that allows application code to interact directly with the runtime system. An example is the Thread class in the Java language, which allows code (that is animated by one thread) to do things such as start and stop other threads. Normally, core aspects of a language's behavior such as task scheduling and resource management are not accessible in this fashion.

Higher-level behaviors implemented by a runtime system may include tasks such as drawing text on the screen or making an Internet connection. It is often the case that operating systems provide these kinds of behaviors as well, and when available, the runtime system is implemented as an abstraction layer that translates the invocation of the runtime system into an invocation of the operating system. This hides the complexity or variations in the services offered by different operating systems. This also implies that the OS kernel can itself be viewed as a runtime system, and that the set of OS calls that invoke OS behaviors may be viewed as interactions with a runtime system.

In the limit, the runtime system may provide services such as a P-code machine or virtual machine, that hide even the processor's instruction set. This is the approach followed by many interpreted languages such as AWK, and some languages like Java, which are meant to be compiled into some machine-independent intermediate representation code (such as bytecode). This arrangement greatly simplifies the task of language implementation and its adaptation to different machines, and improves efficiency of sophisticated language features such as reflection. It also allows the same program to be executed on any machine without an explicit recompiling step, a feature that has become very important since the proliferation of the World Wide Web. To speed up execution, some runtime systems feature just-in-time compilation to machine code.

At the other extreme, the physical CPU itself can be viewed as an implementation of the runtime system of a specific assembly language. In this view, the execution model is implemented by the physical CPU and memory systems. As an analogy, runtime systems for higher-level languages are themselves implemented using some other languages. This creates a hierarchy of runtime systems, with the CPU itself – or actually its inner digital logic structures that determine things like program counter advancement and scheduling of instructions – acting as the lowest-level runtime system.

A modern aspect of runtime systems is parallel execution behaviors, such as the behaviors exhibited by mutex constructs in Pthreads and parallel section constructs in OpenMP. A runtime system with such parallel execution behaviors may be modularized according to the proto-runtime approach.

History

Notable early examples of runtime systems are the interpreters for BASIC and Lisp. These environments also included a garbage collector. Forth is an early example of a language that was designed to be compiled into intermediate representation code; its runtime system was a virtual machine that interpreted that code. Another popular, if theoretical, example is Donald Knuth's MIX computer.

In C and later languages that supported dynamic memory allocation, the runtime system also included a library that managed the program's memory pool.

In the object-oriented programming languages, the runtime system was often also responsible for dynamic type checking and resolving method references.

Runtime Library

In computer programming, a runtime library is a set of low-level routines used by a compiler to invoke some of the behaviors of a runtime environment, by inserting calls to the runtime library into compiled executable binary. The runtime environment implements the execution model, built-in functions, and other fundamental behaviors of a programming language. During execution (run time) of that computer program, execution of those calls to the runtime library cause communication between the executable binary and the runtime environment. A runtime library often includes built-in functions for memory management or exception handling. Therefore, a runtime library is always specific to the platform and compiler.

The runtime library may implement a portion of the runtime environment's behavior, but if one reads the code of the calls available, they are typically only thin wrappers that simply package information, and send it to the runtime environment or operating system. However, sometimes the term *runtime library* is meant to include the code of the runtime environment itself, even though much of that code cannot be directly reached via a library call.

For example, some language features that can be performed only (or are more efficient or accurate) at runtime are implemented in the runtime environment and may be invoked via the runtime library API, e.g. some logic errors, array bounds checking, dynamic type checking, exception handling, and possibly debugging functionality. For this reason, some programming bugs are not discovered until the program is tested in a "live" environment with real data, despite sophisticated compile-time checking and testing performed during development.

As another example, a runtime library may contain code of built-in low-level operations too complicated for their inlining during compilation, such as implementations of arithmetic operations not directly supported by the targeted CPU, or various miscellaneous compiler-specific operations and directives.

The concept of a *runtime library* should not be confused with an ordinary program library like that created by an application programmer or delivered by a third party, nor with a dynamic library, meaning a program library linked at run time. For example, the C programming language requires only a minimal runtime library (commonly called crt0), but defines a large standard library (called C standard library) that has to be provided by each implementation.

Memory Ordering

Memory ordering describes the order of accesses to computer memory by a CPU. The term can refer either to the memory ordering generated by the compiler during compile time, or to the memory ordering generated by a CPU during runtime.

In modern microprocessors, memory ordering characterizes the CPUs ability to reorder memory operations - it is a type of out-of-order execution. Memory reordering can be used to fully utilize the bus-bandwidth of different types of memory such as caches and memory banks.

On most modern uniprocessors memory operations are not executed in the order specified by the program code. In single threaded programs all operations appear to have been executed in the order specified, with all out-of-order execution hidden to the programmer – however in multi-threaded environments (or when interfacing with other hardware via memory buses) this can lead to problems. To avoid problems memory barriers can be used in these cases.

Compile-time Memory Ordering

The compiler has some freedom to resort the order of operations during compile time. However this can lead to problems if the order of memory accesses is of importance.

Compile-time Memory Barrier Implementation

These barriers prevent a compiler from reordering instructions during compile time – they do not prevent reordering by CPU during runtime.

- The GNU inline assembler statement

```
asm volatile("" ::: "memory");
```

or even

```
__asm__ __volatile__ ("" ::: "memory");
```

forbids GCC compiler to reorder read and write commands around it.

- The C11/C++11 command

```
atomic_signal_fence(memory_order_acq_rel);
```

forbids the compiler to reorder read and write commands around it.

- Intel ECC compiler uses "full compiler fence"

```
__memory_barrier()
```

intrinsics.

- Microsoft Visual C++ Compiler:

```
_ReadWriteBarrier()
```

Runtime Memory Ordering

In Symmetric Multiprocessing (SMP) Microprocessor Systems

There are several memory-consistency models for SMP systems:

- Sequential consistency (all reads and all writes are in-order)

- Relaxed consistency (some types of reordering are allowed)

  o Loads can be reordered after loads (for better working of cache coherency, better scaling)

  o Loads can be reordered after stores

- o Stores can be reordered after stores

- o Stores can be reordered after loads

- • Weak consistency (reads and writes are arbitrarily reordered, limited only by explicit memory barriers)

On some CPUs

- • Atomic operations can be reordered with loads and stores.

- • There can be incoherent instruction cache pipeline, which prevents self-modifying code from being executed without special instruction cache flush/reload instructions.

- • Dependent loads can be reordered (this is unique for Alpha). If the processor fetches a pointer to some data after this reordering, it might not fetch the data itself but use stale data which it has already cached and not yet invalidated. Allowing this relaxation makes cache hardware simpler and faster but leads to the requirement of memory barriers for readers and writers.

Memory ordering in some architectures												
Type	Alpha	ARM v7	PA-RISC	POWER	SPARC RMO	SPARC PSO	SPARC TSO	x86	x86 oo-store	AMD 64	IA-64	z/Architecture
Loads reordered after loads	Y	Y	Y	Y	Y				Y		Y	
Loads reordered after stores	Y	Y	Y	Y	Y				Y		Y	
Stores reordered after stores	Y	Y	Y	Y	Y	Y			Y		Y	
Stores reordered after loads	Y	Y	Y	Y	Y	Y	Y	Y	Y	Y	Y	Y
Atomic reordered with loads	Y	Y		Y	Y						Y	
Atomic reordered with stores	Y	Y		Y	Y	Y					Y	
Dependent loads reordered	Y											
Incoherent instruction cache pipeline	Y	Y		Y	Y	Y	Y	Y	Y		Y	

Some older x86 and AMD systems have weaker memory ordering

SPARC memory ordering modes:

- SPARC TSO = total store order (default)

- SPARC RMO = relaxed-memory order (not supported on recent CPUs)

- SPARC PSO = partial store order (not supported on recent CPUs)

Hardware Memory Barrier Implementation

Many architectures with SMP support have special hardware instruction for flushing reads and writes during runtime.

- x86, x86-64

```
lfence (asm), void _mm_lfence(void)
sfence (asm), void _mm_sfence(void)
mfence (asm), void _mm_mfence(void)
```

- PowerPC

```
sync (asm)
```

- MIPS

```
sync (asm)
```

- Itanium

```
mf (asm)
```

- POWER

```
dcs (asm)
```

- ARMv7

```
dmb (asm)
dsb (asm)
isb (asm)
```

Compiler Support for Hardware Memory Barriers

Some compilers support builtins that emit hardware memory barrier instructions:

- GCC, version 4.4.0 and later, has `__sync_synchronize`.

- Since C11 and C++11 an `atomic_thread_fence()` command was added.

- The Microsoft Visual C++ compiler has `MemoryBarrier()`.

- Sun Studio Compiler Suite has `__machine_r_barrier`, `__machine_w_barrier` and `__machine_rw_barrier`.

Runtime Environment

- Relationship between names and data objects (of target machine)

- Allocation & de-allocation is managed by run time support package

- Each execution of a procedure is an activation of the procedure. If procedure is recursive, several activations may be alive at the same time.

- If a and b are activations of two procedures then their lifetime is either non overlapping or nested

- A procedure is recursive if an activation can begin before an earlier activation of the same procedure has ended

When one starts running the program then some data is only available at run time, so we must relate the static source text of a program to the actions that must occur at run time to implement the program. We need to understand the relationship between names and data objects (address and value). Allocation & de-allocation is managed by run time support package which consists of routines loaded with the generated target code. Each execution of a procedure is referred to as an activation of the procedure. If the procedure is recursive, several of its activations may be alive at the same time. We will be dealing with activations of two procedures whose lifetimes are either non overlapping or nested. That is, if a and b are procedure activations and b is entered before a is left, then control must leave b before leaves a. We will not be dealing with partially overlapping activations (threads). A procedure is recursive if a new activation can begin before an earlier activation of the same procedure has ended.

Procedure

- A procedure definition is a declaration that associates an identifier with a statement (procedure body)

- When a procedure name appears in an executable statement, it is called at that point

- Formal parameters are the one that appear in declaration. Actual Parameters are the one that appear in when a procedure is called.

A procedure definition is a declaration that associates an identifier with a statement. The identifier is the procedure name and the statement is the procedure body. Procedures that return value are also referred as procedures so a complete program is also a procedure. When a procedure name appears within an executable statement, the procedure is said to be called at that point. Basically, this procedure call executes the procedure body. The identifiers appearing in the procedure definition are called the formal parameters (or just formals) of the procedure. Arguments, known as actual arguments may be passed to a called procedure, they are substituted for the formal parameters in the procedure body.

Activation Tree

- Control flows sequentially

- Execution of a procedure starts at the beginning of body

- It returns control to place where procedure was called from

- A tree can be used, called an activation tree, to depict the way control enters and leaves activations

- The root represents the activation of main program

- Each node represents an activation of procedure

- The node a is parent of b if control flows from a to b

- The node a is to the left of node b if lifetime of a occurs before b

In our discussion we will make the following assumptions about the flow of control among procedures during the execution of the program:

1. Control flows sequentially: that is, the execution of a program consists of a sequence of steps and the control does not change arbitrarily but only on explicit calls.

2. Each execution of a procedure starts at the beginning of the procedure body and eventually returns control to the point immediately following the place where the procedure was called. A tree like data structure can be used to depict the way control enters and leaves activation this tree is called an activation tree.

3. The root represents the activation of the main program.

4. Each node represents an activation of a procedure.

5. The node for a is the parent of the node for b if and only if control flows from activation a to b.

6. The node for a is to the left of the node for b if and only if the lifetime of a occurs before the lifetime of b.

Example

```
program sort;                          procedure quicksort
    var a : array[0..10] of            (m, n
    integer;
                                       :integer);
                                           var i :integer;
        procedure readarray;                   :
        var i :integer;
            :                          i:= partition (m,n);
                                       quicksort (m,i-1);
        function partition (y, z       quicksort(i+1, n);
                        :integer)
        :integer;                          :
        var i, j ,x, v :integer;       begin{main}
            :                              readarray;
                                           quicksort(1,9)
                                       end.
```

In this example we are only concerned about the declarations and the variables and so the body of the procedures is not mentioned. In the example it is assumed that the value retuned by partition (1,9) is 4.

Activation Tree

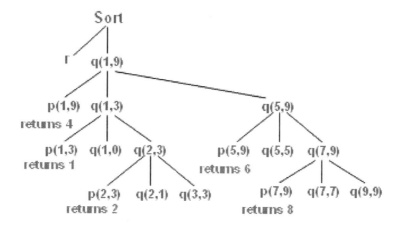

The flow of control of the call quicksort(1,9) would be like

Execution begins..

enter readarray

exit readarray

enter quicksort(1,9)

enter partition(1,9)

exit partition(1,9)

enter quicksort(1,3)

exit quicksort(1,3)

enter quicksort(5,9)

exit quicksort(5,9)

exit quicksort(1,9)

Execution terminates

When the information is represented as an activation tree we get the tree as shown.

Control Stack

- Flow of control in program corresponds to depth first traversal of activation tree
- Use a stack called control stack to keep track of live procedure activations
- Push the node when activation begins and pop the node when activation ends
- When the node n is at the top of the stack the stack contains the nodes along the path from n to the root

The flow of control in a program corresponds to a depth first traversal of the activation tree that starts at the root, visits a node before its children, and recursively visits children at each node in a left to right fashion. A stack called control stack is used to keep track of live procedure activations. The idea is to push the node for an activation onto the control stack as the activation begins and to pop the node when the activation ends. Then the contents of the control stack are related to paths to the root of the activation tree. When node n is at the top of the control stack, the stack contains the nodes along the path from n to the root.

If in the previous example, we consider the activation tree when the control reaches q(2,3), then at this point the control stack will contain the following nodes:

s, q(1,9), q(1,3), q(2,3)

following the path to the root.

Scope of Declaration

- A declaration is a syntactic construct associating information with a name

    - Explicit declaration :Pascal (Algol class of languages) var i : integer

    - Implicit declaration: Fortrani is assumed to be integer

- There may be independent declarations of same name in a program.

- Scope rules determine which declaration applies to a name

- Name binding

$$\text{name} \xrightarrow{\text{environment}} \text{storage} \xrightarrow{\text{state}} \text{value}$$

A declaration in a language is a syntactic construct associating information with a name. There can be two types of declarations

- Explicit declaration : Pascal (Algol class of languages) e.g.- var i : integer.

- Implicit declaration: e.g.,- In Fortran the variable i is assumed to be integer unless declared.

There may be independent declarations of the same name in different parts of a program. The portion of the program to which a declaration applies is called the scope of the declaration. An occurrence of a name in a procedure is said to be local to the procedure if it is in the scope of a declaration within the procedure, or else it is called nonlocal. Scope rules determine which declaration applies to a name.

Storage Organization

The runtime storage might be subdivided into

    - Target code

- Data objects

- Stack to keep track of procedure activation

- Heap to keep all other information

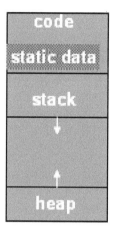

This kind of organization of run-time storage is used for languages such as Fortran, Pascal and C. The size of the generated target code, as well as that of some of the data objects, is known at compile time. Thus, these can be stored in statically determined areas in the memory.

Pascal and C use the stack for procedure activations. Whenever a procedure is called, execution of an activation gets interrupted, and information about the machine state (like register values) is stored on the stack. When the called procedure returns, the interrupted activation can be restarted after restoring the saved machine state.

The heap may be used to store dynamically allocated data objects, and also other stuff such as activation information (in the case of languages where an activation tree cannot be used to represent lifetimes). Both the stack and the heap change in size during program execution, so they cannot be allocated a fixed amount of space. Generally they start from opposite ends of the memory and can grow as required, towards each other, until the space available has filled up.

Activation Record

The activation record is used to store the information required by a single procedure call. Not all the fields shown in the figure may be needed for all languages. The record structure can be modified as per the language/compiler requirements. For Pascal and C, the activation record is generally stored on the run-time stack during the period when the procedure is executing. Of the fields shown in the figure, access link and control link are optional (e.g. Fortran doesn't need access links). Also, actual parameters and return values are often stored in registers instead of the activation record, for greater efficiency. The activation record for a procedure call is generated by the compiler. Generally, all field sizes can be determined at compile time. However, this is not possible in the case of a procedure which has a local array whose size depends on a parameter.

- temporaries: used in expression evaluation

- local data: field for local data

- saved machine status: holds info about machine status before procedure call

- access link : to access non local data

- control link : points to activation record of caller

- actual parameters: field to hold actual parameters

- returned value : field for holding value to be returned

Temporaries
local data
machine status
Access links
Control links
Parameters
Return value

Issues to be Addressed

- Can procedures be recursive?

- What happens to locals when procedures return from an activation?

- Can procedure refer to non local names?

- How to pass parameters?

- Can procedure be parameter?

- Can procedure be returned?

- Can storage be dynamically allocated?

- Can storage be de-allocated?

There are several issues that need to be looked at relating to procedure calls, and they are listed here. All of these are relevant to the design of the runtime system. For instance, the runtime system may have to be designed differently to support recursion. In some cases, local variables may need to be preserved after a procedure returns. Parameter passing may be carried out in multiple ways, such as call by value and call by reference. If storage is dynamically allocated, then a de-allocation mechanism (a garbage collector) may be required.

Layout of Local Data

- Assume byte is the smallest unit

- Multi-byte objects are stored in consecutive bytes and given address of first byte

- The amount of storage needed is determined by its type

- Memory allocation is done as the declarations are processed

- Data may have to be aligned (in a word) padding is done to have alignment.

  - Complier may pack the data so no padding is left

  - Additional instructions may be required to execute packed data

We are assuming here that runtime storage is allocated in blocks of contiguous bytes. As mentioned, type determines the amount of space needed. Elementary types generally require an integral number of bytes. For aggregates like arrays or structures, enough memory is needed to store all their components. This memory is usually allocated contiguously for easy access. As declarations are examined, the space for local data is laid out. A count is kept of the number of allocated memory locations. From this count, a relative address for each local data object can be determined, with respect to some fixed starting point such as the beginning of the activation record. This relative address, or offset, represents the difference between the addresses of the starting point and the data object. The layout of data may be influenced by the machine's addressing system. For example, a machine may have a word of length 4 bytes, and may expect separate data objects to be stored in separate words (i.e., each object should have a starting byte address divisible by 4). In order to achieve this kind of alignment, padding has to be used, which means that blank spaces are left in between objects, with the number of blanks after an object depending on its size. Even if the machine can operate on non- aligned data, it may increase runtime delays, so padding is useful to speed up data access. For example, FORTRAN has a specification for a packed array, which can be declared as follows:

a: packed array [1.10] of boolean;

As per the language specification, this should take up only 10 bits of memory , but it was actually implemented in such a way as to take up 10 words (on a typical machine, each word has 32 bits), because it was too inefficient to store it without padding. Sometimes, due to space constraints, padding may not be possible, so that the data has to be packed together, with no gaps. Since the machine generally expects aligned data, special instructions may be required at runtime to position packed data so that it can be operated on as if aligned.

Storage Allocation Strategies

- Static allocation: lays out storage at compile time for all data objects

- Stack allocation: manages the runtime storage as a stack

- Heap allocation :allocates and de-allocates storage as needed at runtime from heap

These represent the different storage-allocation strategies used in the distinct parts of the runtime memory organization. We will now look at the possibility of using these strategies to allocate memory for activation records. Different languages use different strategies for this purpose. For example, old FORTRAN used static allocation, Algol type languages use stack allocation, and LISP type languages use heap allocation.

Static Allocation

- Names are bound to storage as the program is compiled

- No runtime support is required

- Bindings do not change at run time

- On every invocation of procedure names are bound to the same storage

- Values of local names are retained across activations of a procedure

These are the fundamental characteristics of static allocation. Since name binding occurs during compilation, there is no need for a run-time support package. The retention of local name values across procedure activations means that when control returns to a procedure, the values of the locals are the same as they were when control last left. For example, suppose we had the following code, written in a language using static allocation: function F( )

{

int a;

print(a);

a = 10;

}

After calling F( ) once, if it was called a second time, the value of a would initially be 10, and this is what would get printed.

- Type of a name determines the amount of storage to be set aside

- Address of a storage consists of an offset from the end of an activation record

- Compiler decides location of each activation

- All the addresses can be filled at compile time

- Constraints

  - Size of all data objects must be known at compile time

  - Recursive procedures are not allowed

  - Data structures cannot be created dynamically

The type of a name determines its storage requirement, as outlined. The address for this storage is an offset from the procedure's activation record, and the compiler positions the records relative to the target code and to one another (on some computers, it may be possible to leave this relative position unspecified, and let the link editor link the activation records to the executable code). After this position has been decided, the addresses of the activation records, and hence of the storage for each name in the records, are fixed. Thus, at compile time, the addresses at which the target code can find the data it operates upon can be filled in. The addresses at which information is to be saved when a procedure call takes place are also known at compile time. Static allocation does have some limitations:

- Size of data objects, as well as any constraints on their positions in memory, must be available at compile time.

- No recursion, because all activations of a given procedure use the same bindings for local names.

- No dynamic data structures, since no mechanism is provided for run time storage allocation.

Stack Allocation

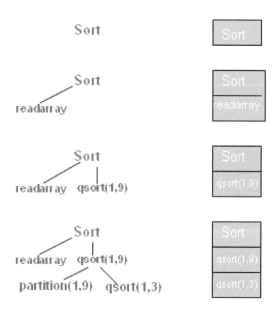

Figure shows the activation records that are pushed onto and popped for the run time stack as the control flows through the given activation tree. First the procedure is activated. Procedure readarray 's activation is pushed onto the stack, when the control reaches the first line in the procedure sort . After the control returns from the activation of the readarray , its activation is popped. In the activation of sort , the control then reaches a call of qsort with actuals 1 and 9 and an activation of qsort is pushed onto the top of the stack. In the last stage the activations for partition (1,3) and qsort (1,0) have begun and ended during the life time of qsort (1,3), so their activation records have come and gone from the stack, leaving the activation record for qsort (1,3) on top.

Calling Sequence

A call sequence allocates an activation record and enters information into its fields. A return sequence restores the state of the machine so that the calling sequence can continue execution. Calling sequence and activation records differ, even for the same language. The code in the calling sequence is often divided between the calling procedure and the procedure it calls. There is no exact division of runtime tasks between the caller and the callee. As shown in the figure, the register stack top points to the end of the machine status field in the activation record. This position is known to the caller, so it can be made responsible for setting up stack top before control flows to the called procedure. The code for the callee can access its temporaries and the local data using offsets from stack top.

- A call sequence allocates an activation record and enters information into its field

- A return sequence restores the state of the machine so that calling procedure can continue execution

- Caller evaluates the actual parameters

- Caller stores return address and other values (control link) into callee's activation record

- Callee saves register values and other status information

- Callee initializes its local data and begins execution

The fields whose sizes are fixed early are placed in the middle. The decision of whether or not to use the control and access links is part of the design of the compiler, so these fields can be fixed at compiler construction time. If exactly the same amount of machine-status information is saved for each activation, then the same code can do the saving and restoring for all activations. The size of temporaries may not be known to the front end. Temporaries needed by the procedure may be reduced by careful code generation or optimization. This field is shown after that for the local data. The caller usually evaluates the parameters and communicates them to the activation record of the callee. In the runtime stack, the activation record of the caller is just below that for the callee. The fields for parameters and a potential return value are placed next to the activation record of the caller. The caller can then access these fields using offsets from the end of its own activation record. In particular, there is no reason for the caller to know about the local data or temporaries of the callee.

Return Sequence

- Callee places a return value next to activation record of caller

- Restores registers using information in status field

- Branch to return address

- Caller copies return value into its own activation record

As described earlier, in the runtime stack, the activation record of the caller is just below that for the callee. The fields for parameters and a potential return value are placed next to the activation record of the caller. The caller can then access these fields using offsets from the end of its own activation record. The caller copies the return value into its own activation record. In particular, there is no reason for the caller to know about the local data or temporaries of the callee. The given calling sequence allows the number of arguments of the called procedure to depend on the call. At compile time, the target code of the caller knows the number of arguments it is supplying to the callee. The caller knows the size of the parameter field. The target code of the called must be prepared to handle other calls as well, so it waits until it is called, then examines the parameter field. Information describing the parameters must be placed next to the status field so the callee can find it.

Long Length Data

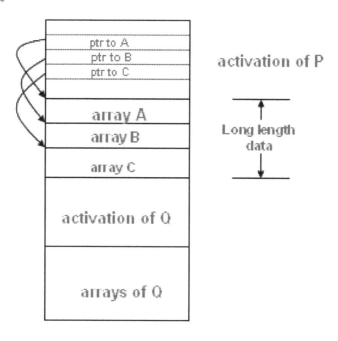

The procedure P has three local arrays. The storage for these arrays is not part of the activation record for P; only a pointer to the beginning of each array appears in the activation record. The relative addresses of these pointers are known at the compile time, so the target code can access array elements through the pointers. Also shown is the procedure Q called by P . The activation record for Q begins after the arrays of P. Access to data on the stack is through two pointers, top and stack top. The first of these marks the actual top of the stack; it points to the position at which the next activation record begins. The second is used to find the local data. For consistency with the organization of the figure, suppose the stack top points to the end of the machine status field. In this figure the stack top points to the end of this field in the activation record for Q. Within the field is a control link to the previous value of stack top when control was in calling activation of P. The code that repositions top and stack top can be generated at compile time, using the sizes of the fields in the activation record. When q returns, the new value of top is stack top minus the length of the machine status and the parameter fields in Q's activation record. This length is known at the compile time, at least to the caller. After adjusting top, the new value of stack top can be copied from the control link of Q.

Dangling References

Referring to locations which have been deallocated

main()

      {int *p;

            p = dangle(); /* dangling reference */

      }

int *dangle();

      {

            int i=23;

            return &i;

      }

The problem of dangling references arises, whenever storage is de-allocated. A dangling reference occurs when there is a reference to storage that has been de-allocated. It is a logical error to use dangling references, since the value of de-allocated storage is undefined according to the semantics of most languages. Since that storage may later be allocated to another datum, mysterious bugs can appear in the programs with dangling references.

Heap Allocation

- Stack allocation cannot be used if:

  - The values of the local variables must be retained when an activation ends

  - A called activation outlives the caller

- In such a case de-allocation of activation record cannot occur in last-in first-out fashion \

- Heap allocation gives out pieces of contiguous storage for activation records

There are two aspects of dynamic allocation -:

- Runtime allocation and de-allocation of data structures.

- Languages like Algol have dynamic data structures and it reserves some part of memory for it.

If a procedure wants to put a value that is to be used after its activation is over then we cannot use stack for that purpose. That is language like Pascal allows data to be allocated under program control. Also in certain language a called activation may outlive the caller procedure. In such a case last-in-first-out queue will not work and we will require a data structure like heap to store the activation. The last case is not true for those languages whose activation trees correctly depict the flow of control between procedures.

- Pieces may be de-allocated in any order

- Over time the heap will consist of alternate areas that are free and in use

- Heap manager is supposed to make use of the free space

- For efficiency reasons it may be helpful to handle small activations as a special case

- For each size of interest keep a linked list of free blocks of that size

Initializing data-structures may require allocating memory but where to allocate this memory. After doing type inference we have to do storage allocation. It will allocate some chunk of bytes. But in language like lisp it will try to give continuous chunk. The allocation in continuous bytes may lead to problem of fragmentation i.e. you may develop hole in process of allocation and de-allocation. Thus storage allocation of heap may lead us with many holes and fragmented memory which will make it hard to allocate continuous chunk of memory to requesting program. So we have heap mangers which manage the free space and allocation and de-allocation of memory. It would be efficient to handle small activations and activations of predictable size as a special case as described. The various allocation and de-allocation techniques used will be discussed later.

- Fill a request of size s with block of size s ' where s ' is the smallest size greater than or equal to s

- For large blocks of storage use heap manager

- For large amount of storage computation may take some time to use up memory so that time taken by the manager may be negligible compared to the computation time

As mentioned earlier, for efficiency reasons we can handle small activations and activations of predictable size as a special case as follows:

1. For each size of interest, keep a linked list if free blocks of that size

2. If possible, fill a request for size s with a block of size s', where s' is the smallest size greater than or equal to s. When the block is eventually de-allocated, it is returned to the linked list it came from.

3. For large blocks of storage use the heap manger.

Heap manger will dynamically allocate memory. This will come with a runtime overhead. As heap manager will have to take care of defragmentation and garbage collection. But since heap manger saves space otherwise we will have to fix size of activation at compile time, runtime overhead is the price worth it.

Access to Non-local Names

- Scope rules determine the treatment of non-local names

- A common rule is lexical scoping or static scoping (most languages use lexical scoping)

The scope rules of a language decide how to reference the non-local variables. There are two methods that are commonly used:

1. Static or Lexical scoping: It determines the declaration that applies to a name by examining the program text alone. E.g., Pascal, C and ADA.

2. Dynamic Scoping: It determines the declaration applicable to a name at run time, by considering the current activations. E.g., Lisp

Block

- Blocks can be nested

- The property is referred to as block structured

- Scope of the declaration is given by most closely nested rule

  - The scope of a declaration in block B includes B

  - If a name X is not declared in B then an occurrence of X is in the scope of declarator X in B ' such that

    ○ B ' has a declaration of X

    ○ B ' is most closely nested around B

Blocks contains its own local data structure. Blocks can be nested and their starting and ends are marked by a delimiter. They ensure that either block is independent of other or nested in another block. That is, it is not possible for two blocks B1 and B2 to overlap in such a way that first block B1 begins, then B2, but B1 end before B2. This nesting property is called block structure. The scope of declaration in a block-structured language is given by the most closely nested rule: 1. The scope of a declaration in a block B includes B. 2. If a name X is not declared in a block B, then an occurrence of X in B is in the scope of a declaration of X in an enclosing block B ' such that . B ' has a declaration of X, and . B ' is more closely nested around B then any other block with a declaration of X.

Example

```
main()
{                        BEGINNING of B0          Scope B0, B1, B3
    int a=0                                        Scope B0
    int b=0
    {                    BEGINNING of B1           Scope B1, B2
        int b=1
        {                BEGINNING of B2           Scope B2
            int a=2
            print a, b
        }                END of B2
                                                   Scope B3
        {                BEGINNING of B3
            int b=3
            print a, b
        }                END of B3
        print a, b
    }                    END of B1
    print a, b
}                        END of B0
```

For the example in the slide, the scope of declaration of b in B0 does not include B1 because b is re-declared in B1. We assume that variables are declared before the first statement in which they are accessed. The scope of the variables will be as follows:

Declaration	Scope
int a=0	B0 not including B2
int b=0	B0 not including B1
int b=1	B1 not including B3
int a =2	B2 only
int b =3	B3 only

The outcome of the print statement will be, therefore:

2 1

0 3

0 1

0 0

Blocks

- Blocks are simpler to handle than procedures
- Blocks can be treated as parameter less procedures
- Use stack for memory allocation
- Allocate space for complete procedure body at one time

a0
b0
b1
a2,b3

There are two methods of implementing block structure:

1. Stack Allocation : This is based on the observation that scope of a declaration does not extend outside the block in which it appears, the space for declared name can be allocated when the block is entered and de-allocated when controls leave the block. The view treat block as a "parameter less procedure" called only from the point just before the block and returning only to the point just before the block.

2. Complete Allocation : Here you allocate the complete memory at one time. If there are blocks within the procedure, then allowance is made for the storage needed for declarations within the books. If two variables are never alive at the same time and are at same depth they can be assigned same storage.

Lexical Scope without Nested Procedures

- A procedure definition cannot occur within another

- Therefore, all non local references are global and can be allocated at compile time

- Any name non-local to one procedure is non-local to all procedures

- In absence of nested procedures use stack allocation

- Storage for non locals is allocated statically

- A non local name must be local to the top of the stack

- Stack allocation of non local has advantage:

    - Non locals have static allocations

    - Procedures can be passed/returned as parameters

In languages like C nested procedures are not allowed. That is, you cannot define a procedure inside another procedure. So, if there is a non- local reference to a name in some function then that variable must be a global variable. The scope of a global variable holds within all the functions except those in which the variables have been re-declared. Storage for all names declared globally can be allocated statically. Thus their positions will be known at compile time. In static allocation, we use stack allocation. Any other name must be a local of the activation at the top of the stack, accessible through the top pointer. Nested procedures cause this scheme to fail because a non-local may then refer to a local of parent variable which may be buried deep in the stack and not at the top of stack. An important benefit of static allocation for non- locals is that declared procedures can freely be passed as parameters and returned as results (a function is passed in C by passing a pointer to it).

Scope with Nested Procedures

```
Program sort;                          procedure quicksort(m,n:integer);
    var a: array[1..n] of integer;         var k,v : integer;
        x: integer;
    procedure readarray;               function partition(y,z:integer):
        var i: integer;                                        integer;
        begin                              var i,j: integer;
                                           begin

        end;                               end;
    procedure exchange(i,j:integer)    begin
        begin

        end;                           begin
        end;
                                       begin

                                       end.
```

The above example contains a program in Pascal with nested procedure sort readarray

exchange

quicksort

partition

Here we apply the most closely nested rule for deciding scoping of variables and procedure names. The procedure *exchange* called by *partition* , is non-local to *partition* . Applying the rule, we first check if exchange is defined within *quicksort* ; since it is not, we look for it in the main program *sort* .

Nesting Depth

- Main procedure is at depth 1

- Add 1 to depth as we go from enclosing to enclosed procedure

Access to Non-local Names

- Include a field 'access link' in the activation record

- If p is nested in q then access link of p points to the access link in most recent activation of q

Nesting Depth : The notion of nesting depth is used to implement lexical scope. The main program is assumed to be at nesting depth 1 and we add 1 to the nesting depth as we go from an enclosing to an enclosed procedure.

Access Links : To implement the lexical scope for nested procedures we add a pointer called an access link to each activation record. If a procedure p is nested immediately within q in the source text, then the access link in an activation record for p points to the access link in the record for most recent activation of q .

The access links for finding storage for non-locals are shown below.

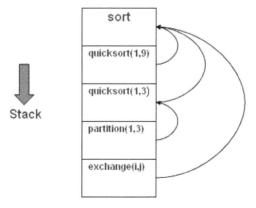

- Suppose procedure p at depth np refers to a non- local *a* at depth na, then storage for *a* can be found as

- follow (np-na) access links from the record at the top of the stack

- after following (np-na) links we reach procedure for which a is local

- Therefore, address of a non local a in procedure p can be stored in symbol table as

  (np-na, offset of a in record of activation having a)

Suppose procedure p at depth np refers to a non-local a with nesting depth na = np. The storage for a can be found as follows:

- When control is in p, an activation record for p is at the top of the stack. Follow the (np - na) access links from the record at the top of the stack.

- After following (np - na) links, we reach an activation record for the procedure that a is local to. As discussed earlier, its storage is at a fixed offset relative to a position in the record. In particular, the offset can be relative to the access link.

The address of non-local a in procedure p is stored as following in the symbol table:

  (np - na, offset within the activation record containing a)

Procedure Parameters

```
program param (input,output);
        procedure b( function h(n:integer): integer);
                begin
                        writeln (h(2))
                end;
procedure c;
                        var m: integer;
                        function f(n: integer): integer;
                begin
                f := m + n
                end;
begin
                m :=0; b(f)
        end;
begin
        c
end.
```

Consider the following program to illustrate the fact that an access link must be passed with the actual parameter f.

- Scope of m does not include procedure b

- within b, call h(2) activates f

- it outputs f(2) which is 2

- how is access link for activation of f is set up?

- a nested procedure must take its access link along with it

- when c passes f:

  - it determines access link for f as if it were calling f

  - this link is passed along with f to b

Lexical scope rules apply even when a nested procedure is passed as a parameter. The scope of declaration of m does not include the body of b. Within the body of b, the call h(2) activates f because the formal h refers to f. Now how to set up the access link for the activation of f? The answer is that a nested procedure that is passed as a parameter must take its access link along with it. When procedure c passes f, it determines an access link for f, just as it would if it were calling f. This link is passed along with f to b. Subsequently, when f is activated from within b, the link is used to set up the access link in the activation record for f.

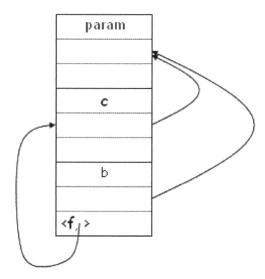

Actual procedure parameter f carries its access link along as described earlier.

Displays

Faster access to non locals than with access links can be obtained using an array d of pointers to activation records, called a display. We maintain display so that storage for a non local a at nesting depth i is in the activation record pointed to by display element d[i].

- Faster access to non locals

- Uses an array of pointers to activation records

- Non locals at depth i is in the activation record pointed to by d[i]

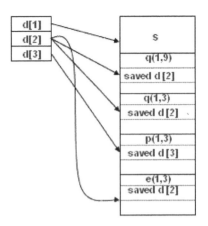

The display changes when a new activation occurs, and it must be reset when control returns from the new activation. When a new activation record for a procedure at nesting depth i is set up, we first save the value of d[i] in the new activation record and then set d[i] to point to the new activation record. Just before an activation ends , d[i] is reset to the saved value.

Justification for Displays

- Suppose procedure at depth j calls procedure at depth i

- Case j < i then i = j + 1

  - called procedure is nested within the caller

  - first j elements of display need not be changed

  - set d[i] to the new activation record

- Case j = i

  - enclosing procedure at depthes 1.i-1 are same and are left un- disturbed

  - old value of d[i] is saved and d[i] points to the new record

  - display is correct as first i-1 records are not disturbed

Suppose procedure at depth j calls procedure at depth i. There are two cases, depending on whether or not the called procedure is nested within the caller in the source text, as in the discussion of access links. 1. Case j < i. Then i = j + 1 and the called procedure is nested within the caller, therefore, the first j elements of display need not be changed, and we set d[i] to the new activation record. The case is illustrated in the figure when sort calls quicksort and also when quicksort calls partition. 2. Case j > i. The enclosing procedure at nesting depths 1,2,.i-1 of the called and calling procedures must be the same and are left un- disturbed. Here the old value of d[i] is saved in the new activation record, and d[i] is pointed to the new record. The display is maintained correctly because first the i-1 records are left as it is.

Dynamic Scope

- Binding of non local names to storage do not change when new activation is set up

- A non local name a in the called activation refers to same storage that it did in the calling activation

In dynamic scope , a new activation inherits the existing bindings of non local names to storage. A non local name a in the called activation refers to the same storage that it did in the calling activation. New bindings are set up for the local names of the called procedure, the names refer to storage in the new activation record.

Dynamic Scoping: Example

- Consider the following program

program dynamic (input, output);

var r: real;

procedure show;

        begin write(r) end;

procedure small;

        var r: real;

        begin r := 0.125; show end;

begin

        r := 0.25;

        show; small; writeln;

        show; small; writeln;

end.

Consider the example shown to illustrate that the output depends on whether lexical or dynamic scope is used.

- Output under lexical scoping

0.250 0.250

0.250 0.250

- Output under dynamic scoping

0.250 0.125

0.250 0.125

The outputs under the lexical and the dynamic scoping are as shown. Under dynamic scoping, when show is called in the main program, 0.250 is written because the variable r local to the main program is used. However, when show is called from within small, 0.125 is written because the variable r local to small is used.

Implementing Dynamic Scope

- Deep Access

  - Dispense with access links

  - use control links to search into the stack

  - term deep access comes from the fact that search may go deep into the stack

- Shallow Access

  - hold current value of each name in static memory

  - when a new activation of p occurs a local name n in p takes over the storage for n

  - previous value of n is saved in the activation record of p

We will discuss two approaches to implement dynamic scope. They bear resemblance to the use of access links and displays, respectively, in the implementation of the lexical scope.

1. Deep Access : Dynamic scope results if access links point to the same activation records that control links do. A simple implementation is to dispense with access links and use control links to search into the stack, looking for the first activation record containing storage for the non- local name. The term deep access comes from the fact that search may go deep into the stack. The depth to which the search may go depends on the input of the program and cannot be determined at compile time.

2. Shallow Access : Here the idea is to hold the current value of each name in static memory. When a new activation of a procedure p occurs, a local name n in p takes over the storage for n. The previous value of n is saved in the activation record for p and is restored when the activation of p ends.

Parameter Passing

- Call by value

  - actual parameters are evaluated and their rvalues are passed to the called procedure

  - used in Pascal and C

  - formal is treated just like a local name

  - caller evaluates the actual parameters and places rvalue in the storage for formals

  - call has no effect on the activation record of caller

This is, in a sense, the simplest possible method of passing parameters. The actual parameters are evaluated and their r-values are passed to the called procedure. Call-by-value is used in C, and Pascal parameters are usually passed this way. Call-by-Value can be implemented as follows:

1. A formal parameter is treated just like a local name, so the storage for the formals is in the activation record of the called procedure.

2. The caller evaluates the actual parameters and places their r-values in the storage for the formals. A distinguishing feature of call-by-value is that operations on the formal parameters do not affect values in the activation record of the caller.

    - Call by reference (call by address)

        - the caller passes a pointer to each location of actual parameters

        - if actual parameter is a name then lvalue is passed

        - if actual parameter is an expression then it is evaluated in a new location and the address of that location is passed

When the parameters are passed by reference (also known as call-by-address or call-by location), the caller passes to the called procedure a pointer to the storage address of each actual parameter.

1. If an actual parameter is a name or an expression having an l-value, then that l-value itself is passed.

2. However, if the actual parameter is an expression, like a + b or 2, that has no l-value, then the expression is evaluated in a new location, and the address of that location is passed.

A reference to a formal parameter in the called procedure becomes, in the target code, an indirect reference through the pointer passed to the called procedure.

    - Copy restore (copy-in copy-out, call by value result)

        - actual parameters are evaluated, rvalues are passed by call by value, lvalues are determined before the call

        - when control returns, the current rvalues of the formals are copied into lvalues of the locals

This is a hybrid form between call-by-value and call-by-reference (also known as copy-in copy-out or value-result).

1. Before control flows to the called procedure, the actual parameters are evaluated. The r-values of the actuals are passed to the called procedure as in call-by-value. In addition, however, the l-values of those actual parameters having l-values are determined before the call.

2. When the control returns, the current r-values of the formal parameters are copied back into the l-values of the actuals, using the l-values computed before the call. Only the actuals having l-values are copied.

    - Call by name (used in Algol)

        - names are copied

        - local names are different from names of calling procedure

swap(i,a[i])

temp = i

i = a[i]

a[i] = temp

This is defined by the copy-rule as used in Algol.

1. The procedure is treated as if it were a macro; that is, its body is substituted for the call in the caller, with the actual parameters literally substituted for the formals. Such a literal substitution is called macro-expansion or inline expansion.

2. The local names of the called procedure are kept distinct from the names of the calling procedure. We can think of each local of the called procedure being systematically renamed into a distinct new name before macro-expansion is done.

3. The actual parameters are surrounded by parentheses if necessary to preserve their integrity.

Language Facility for Dynamic Storage Allocation

- Storage is usually taken from heap

- Allocated data is retained until deallocated

- Allocation can be either explicit or implicit

    - Pascal : explicit allocation and de-allocation by new() and dispose()

    - Lisp : implicit allocation when cons is used, and de- allocation through garbage collection

Static storage allocation is usually done on the stack, as this is a convenient way to take care of the normal scoping rules, where the most recent values have to be considered, and when the scope ends, their values have to be removed. But for dynamic allocation, no such prior information regarding the use of the variables is available. So we need the maximum possible flexibility in this. For this a heap is used. For the sake of a more efficient utilization of memory, the stack grows downwards and the heap grows upwards, starting from different ends of the available memory. This makes sure that all available memory is utilized. Pascal allows for explicit allocation and de-allocation of memory. This can be done by using the new() and dispose() functions. However, in Lisp, continuous checking is done for free memory. When less than 20 percent of the memory is free, then garbage collection is performed. In garbage collection, cells that can no longer be accessed are de-allocated. (Storage that has been allocated but can no longer be accessed is called 'garbage'.)

Dynamic Storage Allocation

Generally languages like Lisp and ML which do not allow for explicit de-allocation of memory do garbage collection. A reference to a pointer that is no longer valid is called a 'dangling reference'. For example, consider this C code:

int main (void)

{

int* a=fun();

```
}
int* fun()
{
int a=3;
int* b=&a;
return b;
}
```

Here, the pointer returned by fun() no longer points to a valid address in memory as the activation of fun() has ended. This kind of situation is called a 'dangling reference'. In case of explicit allocation it is more likely to happen as the user can de-allocate any part of memory, even something that has to a pointer pointing to a valid piece of memory.

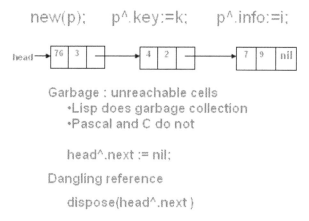

Explicit Allocation of Fixed Sized Blocks

- Link the blocks in a list

- Allocation and de-allocation can be done with very little overhead

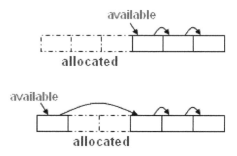

The simplest form of dynamic allocation involves blocks of a fixed size. By linking the blocks in a list, as shown in the figure, allocation and de-allocation can be done quickly with little or no storage overhead.

- blocks are drawn from contiguous area of storage

- An area of each block is used as pointer to the next block

- A pointer available points to the first block

- Allocation means removing a block from the available list

- De-allocation means putting the block in the available list

- Compiler routines need not know the type of objects to be held in the blocks

- Each block is treated as a variant record

Suppose that blocks are to be drawn from a contiguous area of storage. Initialization of the area is done by using a portion of each block for a link to the next block. A pointer available points to the first block. Generally a list of free nodes and a list of allocated nodes is maintained, and whenever a new block has to be allocated, the block at the head of the free list is taken off and allocated (added to the list of allocated nodes). When a node has to be de-allocated, it is removed from the list of allocated nodes by changing the pointer to it in the list to point to the block previously pointed to by it, and then the removed block is added to the head of the list of free blocks. The compiler routines that manage blocks do not need to know the type of object that will be held in the block by the user program. These blocks can contain any type of data (i.e., they are used as generic memory locations by the compiler). We can treat each block as a variant record, with the compiler routines viewing the block as consisting of some other type. Thus, there is no space overhead because the user program can use the entire block for its own purposes. When the block is returned, then the compiler routines use some of the space from the block itself to link it into the list of available blocks.

- Storage can become fragmented

- Situation may arise

  . If program allocates five blocks

  . then de-allocates second and fourth block

      free   free   free

- Fragmentation is of no consequence if blocks are of fixed size

- Blocks can not be allocated even if space is available

In explicit allocation of fixed size blocks, internal fragmentation can occur, that is, the heap may consist of alternate blocks that are free and in use, as shown in the figure. The situation shown can occur if a program allocates five blocks and then de-allocates the second and the fourth, for example. Fragmentation is of no consequence if blocks are of fixed size, but if they are of variable size, a situation like this is a problem, because we could not allocate a block larger than any one of the free blocks, even though the space is available in principle. So, if variable- sized blocks are allocated, then internal fragmentation can be avoided, as we only allocate as much space as we need in a block. But this creates the problem of external fragmentation, where enough space is available in total for our requirements, but not enough space is available in continuous memory locations, as needed for a block of allocated memory. For example, consider another case where we need to allocate 400 bytes of data for the next request, and the available continuous regions of memory that we have are of sizes 300, 200 and 100 bytes. So we have a total of 600 bytes, which is more than what we need. But still we are unable to allocate the memory as we do not have enough contiguous storage. The amount of external fragmentation while allocating variable-sized blocks can become very high on using certain strategies for memory allocation. So we try to use certain strategies for memory allocation, so that we can minimize memory wastage due to external fragmentation.

First Fit Method

- When a block of size s is to be allocated
    - search first free block of size f ≥ s
    - sub divide into two blocks of size s and f-s
    - time overhead for searching a free block
- When a block is de-allocated
    - check if it is next to a free block
    - combine with the free block to create a larger free block

Implicit De-allocation

Implicit deallocation requires cooperation between the user program and run time package, because the latter needs to know when a storage block is no longer in use. This cooperation is implemented by fixing the format of storage blocks. For implicit deallocation it is possible that we periodically make the garbage collector go through each and every link that has been allocated and then try to figure out which are no longer needed. But for efficiency we want that instead of globally considering all the accessible links there are some local tests that can be run on each block to see if it can be deallocated. For this we fix the format of the storage blocks and try to store some extra information to help us more efficiently find whether any given block needs to be deallocated. In spite of these measures, a lot of time is generally wasted on deallocation. For example in Lisp, for sufficiently large programs, around 30 percent of the execution time is spent on garbage collection. While garbage collection is going on, no other execution work can be going on as all links have to be frozen for integrity reasons. So garbage collection greatly slows down execution time, slowing down the production cycle.

- Requires co-operation between user program and run time system
- Run time system needs to know when a block is no longer in use
- Implemented by fixing the format of storage blocks

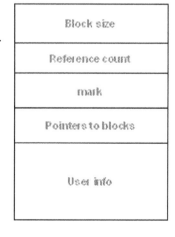

Recognizing Block Boundaries

- If block size is fixed then position information can be used

- Otherwise keep size information to determine the block boundaries

Whether Block is in Use

- References may occur through a pointer or a sequence of pointers

- Compiler needs to know position of all the pointers in the storage

- Pointers are kept in fixed positions and user area does not contain any pointers

While the user program deals with pointers individually, for allocation and de-allocation by the run-time system action must be taken at the level of blocks. That is, a block can be de-allocated only when no pointers are pointing to it. For this, for any pointer we have to keep track of what blocks are being referenced by it. Here we must note that a block can be pointed to differently by a pointer, or the pointer can point to some other pointer, which then points to the block, and so on. For ease in keeping track of this, pointers are kept in fixed positions and the user area does not contain any pointers.

Reference Count

- Keep track of number of blocks which point directly to the present block

- If count drops to 0 then block can be de-allocated

- Maintaining reference count is costly

    - assignment p:=q leads to change in the reference counts of the blocks pointed to by both p and q

- Reference counts are used when pointers do not appear in cycles

One convenient way is to keep track of the number of blocks pointing to any given block. When this number reaches zero, we can see that the block can no longer be reachable and so it has become garbage. This method is easy to implement but can be costly in time as for the assignment p:=q, the reference count of block which was previously pointed to by p goes down by one, while that of q goes up by one. Reference counts are best used when the graph of blocks pointing to blocks is guaranteed to be a forest (can not contain cycles). That is because if there is a cycle, which is not reachable, then the reference count of all blocks in the cycle will be non-zero, even though they are all unreachable. So they will never get de-allocated, thus leading to space wastage.

Marking Techniques

- Suspend execution of the user program

- use frozen pointers to determine which blocks are in use

- This approach requires knowledge of all the pointers

- Go through the heap marking all the blocks unused

- Then follow pointers marking a block as used that is reachable

- De-allocate a block still marked unused

- Compaction: move all used blocks to the end of heap. All the pointers must be adjusted to reflect the move

Marking techniques can be seen as first freezing all activity, and then using an algorithm where you first 'color' all nodes as unused. Then at each pointer, you 'drop down' the color 'used' through links, and all nodes which are colored by this color become marked as 'used'. After this , if a node remains marked as 'unused', then it is truly unused, and can be discarded as garbage. Compaction can be used to save space, but it takes a lot of time as when a block is moved in memory, all pointers pointing to it have to be changed to point to the new location. This also requires us to keep track of all the pointers. The need for compaction is a major problem with variable-sized allotment.

Run Time Storage Management

- Run time allocation and de-allocation of activations occurs as part of procedure call and return sequences

- Assume four kind of statements

call, return, halt and action

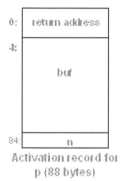

Three address code   Activation record for c (64 bytes)   Activation record for p (88 bytes)

To study the run-time storage management system it is sufficient to focus on the statements: action, call, return and halt, because they by themselves give us sufficient insight into the behavior shown by functions in calling each other and returning. And the run-time allocation and de-allocation of activations occur on the call of functions and when they return. There are mainly two kinds of run-time allocation systems: static allocation and stack allocation. While static allocation is used by the Fortran class of languages, stack allocation is used by the Ada class of languages.

Static Allocation

- A call statement is implemented by a sequence of two instructions

- A move instruction saves the return address

- A goto transfers control to the target code

- The instruction sequence is

  - MOV #here+20, callee.static-area

  - GOTO callee.code-area

- callee.static-area and callee.code-area are constants referring to address of the activation record and the first address of called procedure respectively.

- #here+20 in the move instruction is the return address; the address of the instruction following the goto instruction

- A return from procedure callee is implemented by

GOTO *callee.static-area

For the call statement, we need to save the return address somewhere and then jump to the location of the callee function. And to return from a function, we have to access the return address as stored by its caller, and then jump to it. So for call, we first say: MOV #here+20, callee.static-area. Here, #here refers to the location of the current MOV instruction, and callee.static- area is a fixed location in memory. 20 is added to #here here, as the code corresponding to the call instruction takes 20 bytes (at 4 bytes for each parameter: 4*3 for this instruction, and 8 for the next). Then we say GOTO callee.code-area, to take us to the code of the callee, as callee.codearea is merely the address where the code of the callee starts. Then a return from the callee is implemented by: GOTO *callee.static area. Note that this works only because callee.static-area is a constant.

Example

. Assume each	100: ACTION-l
action	120: MOV 140, 364
block takes 20	132: GOTO 200
bytes of space	140: ACTION-2
.Start address	160: HALT
of code for c	:
and p is	200: ACTION-3
100 and 200	220: GOTO *364
. The activation	:
records	300:
arestatically	304:
allocated starting	:
at addresses	364:
300 and 364.	368:

This example corresponds to the code. Statically we say that the code for c starts at 100 and that for p starts at 200. At some point, c calls p. Using the strategy discussed earlier, and assuming that callee.staticarea is at the memory location 364, we get the code as given. Here we assume that a call to 'action' corresponds to a single machine instruction which takes 20 bytes.

Stack Allocation

- Position of the activation record is not known until run time

- Position is stored in a register at run time, and words in the record are accessed with an offset from the register

- The code for the first procedure initializes the stack by setting up SP to the start of the stack area

MOV #Stackstart, SP

code for the first procedure

HALT

In stack allocation we do not need to know the position of the activation record until run-time. This gives us an advantage over static allocation, as we can have recursion. So this is used in many modern programming languages like C, Ada, etc. The positions of the activations are stored in the stack area, and the position for the most recent activation is pointed to by the stack pointer. Words in a record are accessed with an offset from the register. The code for the first procedure initializes the stack by setting up SP to the stack area by the following command: MOV #Stackstart, SP. Here, #Stackstart is the location in memory where the stack starts.

- A procedure call sequence increments SP, saves the return address and transfers control to the called procedure

ADD #caller.recordsize, SP

MOVE #here+ 16, *SP

GOTO callee.code_area

Consider the situation when a function (caller) calls the another function(callee), then procedure call sequence increments SP by the caller record size, saves the return address and transfers control to the callee by jumping to its code area. In the MOV instruction here, we only need to add 16, as SP is a register, and so no space is needed to store *SP. The activations keep getting pushed on the stack, so #caller.recordsize needs to be added to SP, to update the value of SP to its new value. This works as #caller.recordsize is a constant for a function, regardless of the particular activation being referred to.

- The return sequence consists of two parts.

- The called procedure transfers control to the return address using

GOTO *0(SP)

0(SP) is the address of the first word in the activation record and *0(SP) is the return address saved there.

- The second part of the return sequence is in caller which decrements SP

SUB #caller.recordsize, SP

The value that was referred to by *SP while making the call, is here being referred to as *O(SP). What this means is that the return address previously stored by the caller is now being used by the callee to return back to the caller's code. After this, the caller is removed from the stack by deleting the caller's record size from the stack. So at any point in time, the current activation is not on the stack, but the activations of the function which called it, the function which called that, etc. are on the stack. The code for SUB #caller.recordsize, SP needs to be in the caller, as only the caller has access to #caller.recordsize as a constant.

Example

. Consider the	action-1	/* code for s * /
quicksort	call q	
program	action-2	
. Assume activation	halt	
records for procedures	action-3	/* code for p * /
s, p and q are ssize, psize	return	
and qsize respectively	action-4	/* code for q * /
(determined at compile time)	call p	
.First word in each	action-5	
activation holds the	call q	
return address	action-6	
.Code for the procedures	call q	
start at 100, 200 and	return	
300 respectively, and stack starts at 600.		

s is calling q, q is calling p and q (2 times), p is calling nothing.

100: MOVE #600, SP	300: action-4
108: action-1	320: ADD #qsize, SP
128: ADD #ssize, SP	328: MOVE 344, *SP
136: MOVE 152, *SP	336: GOTO 200
144: GOTO 300	344: SUB #qsize, SP
152: SUB #ssize, SP	352: action-5
160: action-2	372 ADD #qsize, SP
180: HALT	380: MOVE 396, *SP
. . .	388: GOTO 300
	396 SUB #qsize, SP

200: action-3	404: action-6
220: GOTO *o(SP)	424: ADD #qsize, SP
. . .	432: MOVE 448, *SP
	440: GOTO 300
	448: SUB #qsize, SP
	456: GOTO *o(SP)

We assume here that:

The code for s starts at 100.

The code for p starts at 200.

The code for q starts at 300.

The stack area starts at 600.

Code for 'action' takes 20 bytes.

At the beginning, we push 600 to SP so that it points to the start of the stack area. We simplify the strategy outlined earlier. Here we note that 136+16 is 152 (in line 136) and so on in all the MOV instructions at address x, we have written MOV x+16, *SP.

Permissions

We would like to thank the editorial team for lending their expertise to make the book truly unique. They have played a crucial role in the development of this book. Without their invaluable contributions this book wouldn't have been possible. They have made vital efforts to compile up to date information on the varied aspects of this subject to make this book a valuable addition to the collection of many professionals and students.

This book was conceptualized with the vision of imparting up-to-date and integrated information in this field. To ensure the same, a matchless editorial board was set up. Every individual on the board went through rigorous rounds of assessment to prove their worth. After which they invested a large part of their time researching and compiling the most relevant data for our readers.

The editorial board has been involved in producing this book since its inception. They have spent rigorous hours researching and exploring the diverse topics which have resulted in the successful publishing of this book. They have passed on their knowledge of decades through this book. To expedite this challenging task, the publisher supported the team at every step. A small team of assistant editors was also appointed to further simplify the editing procedure and attain best results for the readers.

Apart from the editorial board, the designing team has also invested a significant amount of their time in understanding the subject and creating the most relevant covers. They scrutinized every image to scout for the most suitable representation of the subject and create an appropriate cover for the book.

The publishing team has been an ardent support to the editorial, designing and production team. Their endless efforts to recruit the best for this project, has resulted in the accomplishment of this book. They are a veteran in the field of academics and their pool of knowledge is as vast as their experience in printing. Their expertise and guidance has proved useful at every step. Their uncompromising quality standards have made this book an exceptional effort. Their encouragement from time to time has been an inspiration for everyone.

The publisher and the editorial board hope that this book will prove to be a valuable piece of knowledge for students, practitioners and scholars across the globe.

Index

9 781635 496772